The Guidance Groove

Escape Unproductive Habits,
Trust Your Intuition,
and Be True

CAROLYN KURLE, PhD

The Guidance Groove: Escape Unproductive Habits, Trust Your Intuition, and Be True

Copyright © 2023 by Carolyn M. Kurle, Ph.D.

Published by Treehouse by the Sea Press
Encinitas, California

Editor: Mary L. Holden
Cover design: Kara Reynolds and Anugito ten Voorde of Artline Graphics
Cover art: Kara Reynolds
Interior design: Anugito ten Voorde of Artline Graphics
Interior art: Kara Reynolds
Author photo: J. Stanley Vegar

Printed in: USA
ISBN: (hardback): 979-8-9873418-0-3
ISBN: (paperback): 979-8-9873418-1-0
ISBN: (ebook): 979-8-9873418-4-1
ISBN: (audiobook): 979-8-9873418-2-7
LCNN: 2022921771

To my dad, Don Kurle,
who helped edit an early draft of this book,
and whose acceptance, love, encouragement,
and connection with guidance inspires me still.

To my mom, Martha Cantwell,
whose unfailing love
created and sustains the foundation
from which I fly free.

CONTENTS

PART 1

The Guidance Groove

But I do know what bliss is:
that deep sense of being present,
of doing what you absolutely must do
to be yourself.

Joseph Campbell,
comparative mythology and religion professor

Have the courage to follow your heart and intuition.
They somehow know what you truly want to become.

Steve Jobs,
co-founder, Apple, Inc.

It's 2004 and a four-hour firefight against the U.S. government head-quarters in Najaf, Iraq is in full swing. My friend Chris White, a retired SEAL Team Six Operator turned Team Leader of a civilian contract security force, is there commanding a small group of contractors and soldiers to repel an attack on the headquarters by hundreds of Iraqi militants. In the midst of AK-47 and M-4 gunfire and numerous rocket-propelled grenades and mortar rounds, Chris was responsible for the safety of many civilians, contractors, and military personnel. Those people lived through the day in large part due to the actions of Chris and his team.

When I asked how he made his decisions during a time of extreme life-or-death stress, Chris said that when he is in a combat zone, he relies on his instincts. There is no thinking, only instincts informing actions arising from his years of training. Chris's years of military preparation in the SEAL Teams had created within him a comprehensive set of conditioned responses so when faced with a true fight, flight, or freeze situation, he was able to act effectively from his instincts (what he calls his "Spidey-sense") while also trusting the automatic behaviors that arose from his extensive training.

Animal instincts, such as bird migration, create behaviors which are done without having been taught, and they are thought to have evolved from ancestors who learned a particular behavior and passed that knowledge to the next generations in their DNA through a process known as intergenerational epigenetics. The mechanism by which instincts become ingrained within an animal's DNA is not yet known, but the evidence for the existence of instinctual response is myriad and scientists are working to discover how the neural circuitry in animals governs this intuitive guidance. Chris's instincts pushed him to survive, while his deep, hard-won training provided him quick access to the behaviors necessary to survive and to excel at his job of protecting others.

You are an animal, a human mammal, and you also receive information from your instincts or intuition that can guide your actions. Thankfully, most humans never experience true life or death situations that require a deeply ingrained trained response led by our instinct to survive. But the same principles for relying upon your instincts for navigating life-threatening firefights apply when you face everyday life decisions.

You can learn to rely on your intuition to guide you. You can train yourself to trust your instincts, thereby creating a deep groove of guidance from which you can authentically respond when confronted with everything that greets you throughout your day-to-day life. When you choose to live by your personal guidance, you create new response patterns that reflect your own authenticity, and you then experience greater peace, ease, contentment, and joy.

This is the Guidance Groove.

CHAPTER 1

An Invitation
to Live Within
Your Guidance Groove

The spiritual task we are given is a simple one:
to attend to the inner spark of radiance,
to hold vigil over it until we realize it to be ourself,
and to dig up and cast off all arguments
we have with its love.

Adyashanti, spiritual teacher

What are Grooves?

In the physical world, grooves are created and sustained when repeated action makes a valley across a surface. Imagine riding your bicycle on the same soft surface day after day, your tires building increasing depressions in the dirt. As those indentations deepen over time, they develop into ruts, and it becomes increasingly difficult to diverge or escape when you and your bicycle are caught in them.

In that same way, you create and sustain behavior grooves by habitually following patterns that wear paths across your life. These *Unproductive Grooves* hold you in place, prevent your connection to true guidance, and narrowly dictate your interactions with the world. Adherence to these grooves diminishes your authenticity, contentment, ease, and true happiness.

Grooves are also created when you lose yourself in joyful movement, usually guided by musical rhythms. You can create and deepen this type of groove, a liberated behavior groove, a free and joyful dance through life that is continuously inspired by the music of your own guidance: your own personal *Guidance Groove*.

This book is a tool that shows you how.

Steps for Creating and Sustaining Your Guidance Groove

Recognize there is a choice before you.

Set your objective to choose an outcome
rooted in benevolent intentionality.

Identify the path arising from your
source of true guidance.

Trust your guidance
and choose your actions accordingly.

If you miss the mark,
learn from your experience,
and try again.

To some degree, you already know the steps outlined above. When a decision is required, some part of you wants to act from true guidance and make choices that protect your "inner spark of radiance," as Adyashanti says in the quote above. You want always to be in alignment with your own radiance, your genuine truth. You yearn to create outcomes that maximize the good in your life and create sustained authenticity, ease, and happiness. Yet you see that contentment, freedom, and joy—in your life and in the lives of those you cherish—are often fleeting.

It does not have to be that way. Every single human has that inner spark of radiance or a source of true internal guidance. Over time, your spark can become encrusted, hidden beneath layers of false stories, ideas, and beliefs that deepen and harden your Unproductive Grooves. It feels difficult to find, listen to, and make decisions in alignment with the guidance available from the unencumbered, brilliant light at the source of your being.

The key is to recognize when your false stories create behaviors that fit with the Unproductive Grooves, consciously cast aside those inauthentic stories and behaviors, connect with your source of guidance, and make choices based on the wisdom constantly emanating from your ever-growing Guidance Groove.

This book shows you how to uncover, connect with, and continually groove to the guidance arising from your own inner source of radiance.

Sources of Guidance

Where does intuitive guidance come from? We have yet to discover this, but sources of true guidance have been described by humanity using many names and forms, each reflecting particular cultural and personal experiences. These descriptors allow you to better understand what your source of guidance might be.

These descriptors include:
    Intuition
    Instinct
    Spidey-sense
    Gut feeling
    Sixth sense

Inner voice
Awareness
True self
Stillness
Flow
Spirit
God
Love
Light
Truth
Reality
Buddha Nature
The Universe
The Divine

And there are many more—from across all of humanity.

The names for your true guidance matter less than the way you recognize and build access to your own source, then call upon that source to make choices within a framework of *benevolent intentionality*. Benevolent intentionality means setting your intentions for the best and highest good for everyone. Every single decision must be rooted within this framework. Decisions made outside of benevolent intentionality can lead to outcomes that may appear to benefit you but are perhaps not the best for you or those around you. For example, if you choose to consistently interfere with your child's choices, you may seem to be benefitting their well-being, but you may actually be stifling their creativity, creating a barrier for communication, and developing within your own child a mistrust of their personal decision-making skills.

When you follow your guidance from within a framework of benevolent intentionality, you achieve outcomes that place you on your best and highest pathways. You can then pay attention to those outcomes, and learn to better recognize and trust the physical, mental, and intuitive confirmations of your guidance.

In your daily life, following guidance from within a framework of benevolent intentionality allows you access to your own unique blueprint for authenticity. Your choices then become expressions of your truth—your authenticity—and that's when you experience a graceful path of freedom. This freedom allows for greater personal expansion, satisfaction, and happiness. What is more, navigating life in alignment with your own Guidance Groove creates a positive feedback loop: the more authentic you become, the more your true self is naturally drawn to outcomes for the best and highest good for all, which increases adherence to your Guidance Groove.

What Does it Feel Like to Listen to and Follow Your Guidance?

Once you learn to recognize and cultivate your own guidance, you will understand what it feels like to follow direction from that place of internal awareness. When faced with a decision, big or small, you'll feel an insistence to choose one particular outcome. When you choose otherwise, you'll feel discomfort.

In my own experience, I sometimes picture my source of guidance as a lake that lies within the landscape of my chest and abdomen. When my choices are in alignment with my own benevolent intentionality, with the natural flow of my being, then my lake is calm, without a ripple of discontent. I feel that calm in my physical body and my mental space. Small disturbances mar the surface of my lake when I am slightly off on a choice, and I feel physical, mental, and emotional discomfort. Larger departures from my guidance cause waves to rise and disrupt my lake. I am unable to be with even the minor discomfort of ripples for long, so when I feel any disturbance, I spend more time connecting to my guidance and collecting more data. For example, I may use the logical part of my brain to ask questions and I gather information that helps me better understand why I'm feeling out of alignment. Then, I refine my choice, regain my equilibrium, and smooth my lake's surface.

In other instances, when a decision is presented, I may be hit with a full body *yes* or *no* and these signals are strong, clear, and very difficult to ignore. For example, when I saw my former husband, Christian, for the first time. The immediate intuitive guidance was so strong that to ignore it would have brought extreme discomfort. I even heard a voice in my head saying, "Your life as you know it is over." We married, had our son, and, despite our divorce, which was also precipitated by a full body *yes*, we remain extremely close, and the three of us are a very tight knit, albeit unusual, family.

The Bicycle Ride:
What Does Following Guidance *Feel* Like?

It's 5:30 am and I'm gliding through the dark on my beloved bicycle. This is my time to feel more deeply into my guidance.

As I ride, I open myself to whatever may arise that requires my attention. I invite thoughts and feelings to float through my awareness, waiting for one to pull harder on my attention than the others.

Sometimes nothing arises.

Most times, something comes to the surface with gentle insistence, and I encourage my being to focus on that.

This particular morning, I'm wondering about my dad's funeral. It's coming up soon and I think I want to talk about him during the service, to honor him, to remember him. His funeral was postponed due to COVID-19 fears, so he will have been dead for 10 months by the time the service arrives. My questions flow. Should I speak at my dad's funeral? What should I say? What stories would best invite insight into my dad?

When I ask, "Should I speak at my dad's funeral?" I create different scenarios in my brain as vividly as possible, then I *feel* what it would be like to experience each outcome.

First, I picture myself in front of everyone, talking about my dad, and, with curiosity and care, I examine the feelings that arise. Am I scared? Am I happy? Am I too sad to effectively speak? Do I feel a connection with my dad and with those who are there to remember him? Is my presence as a speaker welcomed by others? Do my stories honor my dad? Am I speaking because I feel obligated as his daughter? Am I speaking because I want the attention?

As I continue to imagine myself speaking at my dad's funeral, I notice that I feel a little nervous and a little fearful of judgment. I also feel abundant love for and from my dad and happiness that I am lucky enough to have had this human in my life in such a special capacity. I feel proud that I am brave enough to publicly declare my love for him. I feel acceptance from my family and friends who support me and who also love my dad. The overwhelming feelings I experience as I imagine the scenario of being a speaker at my dad's memorial service are positive. Before I fully leave this invented situation, I delve more deeply into the small fears. Do they arise from something real? Or are they imaginary stories with little basis in reality?

Then, I picture the opposite scene, me sitting in the audience watching other speakers, choosing to remain silent and safe. And I feel into that experience.

After immersing myself in both, I have a clearer picture: I *feel* better, more at ease, and happier with myself if I choose to speak for and about my dad. I recognize that the slight nervousness I feel as I picture myself in front of everyone reflects my own fears of being inadequate to the task. So, the answer to the first question is *yes*—I will speak at my dad's service. It simply *feels* better than not speaking.

From there, I allow the next question to surface, I picture all the scenarios vividly in my head, and feel into my entire self to see what outcome brings the most ease, the most calmness, the biggest full body *yes*. Or *no*.

I do this for every single decision in my life.

Sometimes I must picture the scenarios many times, across multiple bicycle rides, before I get the clearest answers. Sometimes I realize I need to discuss it with a trusted confidant or use my logical self to do some more research into the facts of what I'm facing to better understand why my intuition is guiding me one way or another. Many more times, my decisions are near immediate, requiring very little time to create and weigh multiple scenarios because I have grown so used to relying on and trusting my guidance. A choice arises, I feel into it, then decide within seconds. If I need more time, I ask for it, hoping to prevent any fears from driving my choices before I have a chance to feel my guidance.

This is the experience of living within one's own Guidance Groove.

Listening to one's own guidance from within a framework of benevolent intentionality requires a degree of detachment from the actual outcome. Guidance that serves the best and highest good may not provide the outcomes that make you, or everyone around you, initially very happy. But choices rooted in benevolent intentionality and genuine personal guidance do provide outcomes that bring the most comfort, ease, and clarity at your deepest level. With time and practice, you'll notice that when you act in ways that are opposite to what your guidance tells you, your personal discomfort becomes increasingly apparent and untenable. Feeling this discomfort when you ignore your guidance will help nudge you back onto the right path. In the end, it's not about making the choice that will satisfy the most people, it's about doing what is authentically in alignment with your guidance. Guidance that supports your own authenticity disregards outside pressures created from inauthentic sources. It is only concerned with the best and highest good.

When it was time for my husband and I to divorce, my guidance to do so was extremely strong but I still had to find the courage to end the marriage and navigate all the difficulty associated with mourning the loss of what we had expected when we married. None of that was nearly as hard as it would have been had I chosen to ignore my guidance to end the marriage. The discomfort, physical and mental, would have been so strong as to make us all miserable. Luckily, my former spouse also listens to his own guidance, and we have recreated, grown, and maintained a new vision of our family unit with much more love, friendship, happy co-parenting, and closeness than if we had remained married.

These are examples from my own life, but when you pay attention to the language you and others use to describe feeling intuitive guidance, you will recognize familiar patterns that you have likely already experienced. People say, "It just felt right," and "I just knew it was supposed to be that way," and "Anything else felt terrible," or "My decision made no logical sense, but I *knew* it was the correct decision."

These phrases occur over and over in conversation, literature, movies, songs, and spiritual teachings, underscoring that each of us experiences moments of true, clear, unambiguous guidance. The universality of the concept of guidance across so many platforms teaches us that the processes driving the Guidance Groove philosophy and lifestyle are always accessible to you. Always.

Once you become more comfortable recognizing, trusting, and following your guidance, then continual application of the Guidance Groove to all aspects of your life will create and sustain authenticity. Acting from authenticity enhances freedom.

And freedom is the ability to make choices based in truth and love, not fear.

Fear is what drives the inauthentic voices that try to influence your decisions. Trust in guidance requires accepting most fears are false. Establishing benevolent intentionality, paying attention to your guidance, then trusting the decisions arising from your guidance will take practice as does learning to interpret guidance in a spectrum of fear

I invite you to identify your authentic self, to find and trust your inner guidance, to create a personal dance to a new groove that leads you to increased ease, peace, freedom, and more joy.

You are ready.

I also invite you to welcome and support others as they develop their own Guidance Grooves. You can encourage freedom for everyone.

CHAPTER 2

Recognize the Unproductive Grooves and Begin Choosing Guidance

In your efforts to avoid fear and pain, you make choices from familiar, known, and comfortable grooves, even when those decisions go against your inner guidance and highest truth. When you ignore guidance from your own authenticity, you feel miserable. You may have happy moments, but continual contentment is impossible. Although you may be at peace and successful in some areas of your life, following the seemingly simple steps put forth in the Guidance Groove can seem difficult when you are mired in Unproductive Grooves across other parts of your life.

But do you want to know something wonderful? Research from the field of psychology repeatedly demonstrates that living an authentic life is positively correlated with optimal functioning, fulfillment, subjective vitality, and life satisfaction. And the positive associations between authenticity and multiple measures of well-being exist across many life arenas such as work, personal relationships, and intrinsic self-esteem. In addition, living outside of your own authenticity is linked to increased distress, depression, stress, anxiety, and unhappiness.

According to the research, authentic living is defined as trusting your inner instincts and operating in harmony with those feelings. Authenticity arises when you consistently act in ways that are in alignment with the guidance from your "true self." Making small and large life choices, and otherwise engaging with the wider world in ways that are consistently aligned with your highest truth, will make you happier. The data are abundantly clear: Intentionally anchoring your choices within your own personal Guidance Groove will increase your overall authenticity which leads to expanded ease, contentment, and abiding happiness.

Why, then, do you have difficulty making choices that lead to greater freedom, contentment, happiness, and joy? Why does humanity continually choose pathways that support struggle and discontent?

It is a human desire to avoid obvious discomfort. Therefore, you choose the familiar and known. You create stories, or Unproductive Grooves, that support your decisions to remain in comfortable, known realities. Often, those around you reinforce your stories and further cloud your ability to connect with your authentic self, follow your true guidance, and step out of your familiar, but ultimately unhelpful, grooves. In living within your Unproductive Grooves, you function on autopilot, ignoring your authentic urges to choose options in alignment with your guidance.

When you live within Unproductive Grooves by ignoring intuition and making choices from fear, you miss the experience of deep relief which is a by-product of living in alignment with your inner guidance.

The Four Unproductive Grooves that Prevent You From Dancing to Your Guidance Groove

I have identified four Unproductive Grooves in which you become trapped to different degrees across multiple arenas of life. There are many behaviors and personalities within each groove, but the flavors among those variations remain consistent with each groove's overall theme. The Unproductive Grooves are outlined briefly below and are addressed more deeply in subsequent chapters.

The Inadequacy Groove is built when you believe happiness relies on your perfection. This groove is deepened by fear that others will discover your perceived deficiencies. To prevent discovery of your flaws, you direct attention away from yourself by creating external, diversionary dramas, or pointing toward other people's inadequacies. You try to maintain control of everything and everyone around you. You may practice harsh self-criticism and constantly reprimand yourself for your perceived failures. Your self-directed harshness can lead to your regular denigration of others as well.

The Obligation Groove forms when your actions stem from a sense of guilt or duty. Creation of this groove is powered by fear that others will perceive your authentic choices as selfish or hurtful. You also fear your perceived value will diminish unless you commit to overextending yourself. You strive to maintain the status quo, using your perceived obligations, your desire to avoid upsetting others, and your need to remain invaluable as excuses to ignore your own guidance toward your true path.

The Scarcity Groove materializes when you believe in a lack of resources such as money, love, power, recognition, or appreciation. You fear others will take your share, so you do all you can to grasp at those resources. Your beliefs in scarcity can lead to needy behaviors within relationships, choosing an unhappy career path motivated only by earning potential, or demonizing others you perceive as threatening your share of a resource.

The Unworthy Groove appears when you are convinced you have little to no inherent value and you are afraid of the intense shame you will experience if others discover your worthlessness. You believe you are not good enough for a rewarding job, friends, a meaningful intimate partnership, or a place of acceptance within your family and community.

The Five Life Arenas Within Which the Four Unproductive Grooves Manifest

There are five main areas in life—your life arenas—in which behaviors associated with the Unproductive Grooves can arise. Reflect on these arenas as you consider the ways Unproductive Groove behaviors can manifest in your own life.

School/Work/Life-path: This is the arena in which you educate yourself and/or make your living, plus the pastimes you pursue to make money, run a household, raise your family, further your education, or otherwise engage in your passions. This arena is populated by those with whom you interact as you make yourself useful on the planet.

Family: Family contains multiple role players and, in the context of this book, includes parents, stepparents, children, siblings, and extended family such as grandparents, aunts, uncles, cousins, and so forth. These are people related by blood or blood-like ties (foster, adoptive, step, legal). Three specific categories are highlighted below because the parent/child and sibling familial relationships are especially powerful.

Parent to Child: There are several stages in which parents interact with their children. These include babies, toddlers, small children, adolescents, and adults. The behaviors from different Unproductive Grooves may manifest at different times throughout the long life of the parent to child relationship. Pay attention to which stage is applicable to your situation.

Grown Child to Parent: This refers to an adult child who is no longer entirely dependent upon the parent.

Siblings: These are people with whom you share biological, adopted, foster, or step-parents. You may have been raised together or apart, but by some way, you are related to or experienced the same familial ties while growing up in similar generations.

Close Intimate Relationship: The non-family people with whom you share physical and emotional intimacy, love, and desire. You may call them by the titles of: spouse, lover, partner, sweetheart, fiancé, girl-friend, boyfriend, or significant other.

Friendship: The people you like, love, and care about with whom you share casual relationships during free time, or on shared interests. Friends are usually different from close intimate partners, acquaintances, or co-workers.

Community: Those with whom you choose to contribute time in your life as a neighbor, volunteer, activist, church member, recreation group participant, local business supporter, etc.

Initial Steps to Free Yourself from Unproductive Grooves

How do you navigate the world without Unproductive Grooves dictating your decisions? Fears driving these grooves are deeply rooted and have a strong gravitational pull. To break their influence requires effort and commitment.

First, identify your Unproductive Grooves. Determine which patterns of your life fit within the four Unproductive Grooves. Recognize and examine the fears driving your attachments to these grooves. Different grooves may resonate with you for different aspects of your life. You may be stuck in the Scarcity Groove in your work arena, but the Inadequacy Groove dominates your close intimate partnership. Perhaps you have a very shallow Obligation Groove in your friendship arena but are deeply embedded in the Unworthy Groove when navigating your community relationships. The chapters with detailed descriptions of the different flavors within the four Unproductive Grooves will help you better understand how adherence to false beliefs prevents you from living within your Guidance Groove.

Second, value your guidance. This is imperative. Following your intuitive self requires feeling into your body to discover and experience what your guidance is telling you. It requires checking in with your entire self, not remaining stuck only in the mental realm. Think back to Chris's story, the former Navy SEAL at the beginning of the book, in the combat zone, following his "Spidey-sense" to act in ways that would save himself and those around him while under hostile fire. To be most effective, Chris chose his actions in response to the continual instinctual input he felt within his entire being. He based each decision on these feelings, the sensory feedback from his most basic instincts to survive and protect. With experience, he learned to completely trust those instincts and he followed them implicitly.

Interestingly, Chris also feels his instincts in more commonplace situations, outside of combat. When looking back at a relationship with a former beloved, he shared with me that his intuition told him at the very start of that relationship it would never work for the long-term because he felt strongly she would never learn to trust him. But she was also beautiful, strong, intelligent, and fun, so he focused on her positive attributes and went into the relationship anyway, only to learn after many years, when they parted ways, that his initial assessment was exactly right. Why had he trusted his guidance in a life-or-death combat zone, but ignored it when choosing to enter a close intimate relationship?

Humans tend to place greater value on tangible characteristics arising from the mental realm, such as cleverness, will, logic, hard work, action, perseverance, and material outcomes. We place less value on the more descriptive aspects of our humanity, such as feelings, emotions, and all the processes by which we access our true guidance.

When your intuition tells you one thing (this relationship won't work out), but your mental realm tells you another story that seems to make sense (they are interesting/smart/beautiful/compelling in some way, so of course the relationship is worth pursuing!), then it's easy to ignore guidance.

Instead of ignoring your guidance when decisions arise, pay attention, notice, and assess the balance between thoughts from your mental realm and sensations from your feeling and emotional aspects. Imbalance among these inputs contributes to remaining stuck in your Unproductive Grooves. When you rely solely on your mental realm, you fractionate your innate wholeness and cut off access to all the useful and informative sensations from your feeling self. However, when you assign a high value to your guidance, and integrate it into your decision-making processes, then you will increasingly recognize how adherence to your truths continually leads to authenticity, liberation, and joy and that will help you to more frequently and automatically notice, welcome, and ultimately trust your guidance.

Third, create more opportunities to connect with your own authentic guidance. Once you assign value to your guidance, then you can establish regular occasions and activities that will enable you to best access your guidance. Discover where and how you most easily connect to your guidance and cultivate the time to create situations to support whatever enhances that connection. Many find meditation useful for tuning into their vast internal truth and intuition. Some find connection to true guidance intensifies with immersion in nature or with movement, such as walking, doing yoga, running, rowing, or cycling. Find what works for you and make time for it.

Fourth, ask for help. Enlist others in your quest to break free of your Unproductive Grooves. Share your intentions with those who love you and in whom you trust. Explain the ways in which your behaviors mirror those described within the four Unproductive Grooves. Express your desire to reject actions arising from fear, instead embracing choices based on authentic guidance.

Asking for help makes you vulnerable which can inspire fear. In the same vein, creating and living within your own Guidance Groove and acting from authenticity requires courage which, according to Brené Brown and many others, does not exist without fear. Courage and fear go hand in hand. Asking for help is courageous and your bravery can vanquish your fear.

A note on this: When asking for help, do so sincerely, with a desire only to receive loving, benevolent, creative support from those who love you. Do not allow others to point accusatory fingers at you when you act from within one of the Unproductive Grooves. When others try to shame you into change, it will not work. Accept only loving help and encouragement. Conversely, do not ask for help in the hopes that your loved ones will read this book and change themselves to better suit you. You are on your journey. Let them discover theirs.

Once you recognize how your behaviors fit within the four Unproductive Grooves, you can identify how every action in life is a choice: A choice to remain in your fear-driven, Unproductive Grooves, or step into your authentic self. Then you will learn to cultivate and connect with your highly valued guidance and make choices more in alignment with your own truth and authenticity.

You are ready to approach life from within your own Guidance Groove.

Choosing the Guidance Groove

As mentioned earlier, interacting with the world from a place of genuine authenticity is strongly linked to multiple measures of well-being. As you move through your life, you have the power to continually make choices that are in alignment with your own personal truth and authentic self and these choices will influence your enduring personal happiness.

This is so important: You have the power to act from your own authenticity which naturally expands your happiness.

And the Guidance Groove is a tool to help you accomplish that expansion.

To start, when you dance to your own Guidance Groove, you realize every single event in life involves a choice. And decisions made when you are in your Guidance Groove are not driven by fear. Instead, you choose actions and outcomes allowing you to remain true to your own authenticity. You actively set your intentions and root your choices within a consideration of the best and highest good. You notice, listen for, feel, and follow your authentic guidance arising from that place of benevolent intentionality.

When you ignore your initial intuitive guidance about a person or situation, and choose to act against that guidance, you must pay attention to the subsequent experiences to confirm or refute your initial intuition, then reassess your initial choice. In this way, you gather data to better trust your initial guidance more quickly.

When you make choices in alignment with your authentic guidance, then happiness, contentment, and liberation follow.

Joanna and Simon: Learning from Experiences to Trust Your Guidance

A dear friend, Joanna, is excited as she has recently met Simon through a dating app. Simon is handsome, successful, active, witty, and eager to meet Joanna. Her travel schedule precludes an in-person meeting for a couple of weeks, but they text multiple times a day after meeting online, declaring their mutual interest and sharing intimate details about their lives. He even removes his profile from the dating site, underscoring his laser focus on Joanna, and she is thrilled.

Joanna is finally scheduled to meet Simon for dinner, and, earlier that day, she and I meet up. She excitedly discusses the long, flirtatious, and very frequent texts exchanged between her and Simon, expressing her eagerness to finally meet him in person to assess their further compatibility. I am beyond happy for her.

However, after sharing her enthusiasm, Joanna sobers a bit. She shows me elements of the text messages indicating Simon has the potential to be excessively possessive. The messages are not extreme, nor even a guaranteed red-flag, but Joanna's intuition is clear, and she articulates her feelings that this early suggestion of possessiveness could eventually lead to a more full-blown problem if Simon's insecurity-fueled inclinations escalate into overly controlling and jealous behaviors. I agree with Joanna's gut instincts, and we talk about how best to move forward with the knowledge that, if these early indications are real, then Simon's behaviors would only get worse.

She agrees it is best to proceed with caution, but since he has so many good qualities, she chooses to meet Simon in person to get more information.

Joanna falls in love with Simon, and they have many adventures, loving and joyful experiences, trips, and the intimate everyday life interactions one experiences with a sweetheart. But also, almost immediately, Joanna is faced with increasing examples of Simon's insecurities regarding her fidelity and commitment to him and their relationship. He badgers her for attention when she is away on work trips, berates her for behavior he deems inappropriate, such as talking at a party (in front of him) about a long-ago ex-boyfriend with whom she had spent time exploring a region of the country of interest to other partygoers. He questions her loyalty, nit-picking and correcting aspects of her behavior that Simon thinks mean Joanna is thinking more of her former or future lovers than him. Simon wants them to sell their respective houses and buy a home together, but something in Joanna resists. As she explains to me, it just doesn't feel right.

Finally, the behaviors escalate to a point that Joanna can't bear the discomfort. They try counseling and many other avenues, but to no avail. Simon simply never believes that Joanna is truly loyal, so despite his many outstanding attributes, she finally listens to her guidance and ends their relationship. She is heart-broken, but also relieved to be done.

In relating to Simon, Joanna has tendencies, in varying degrees, to experience behaviors arising from the Scarcity and Obligation Grooves when navigating intimate partnerships. She feels she is running out of time to meet and establish a long-term, meaningful partnership as she enters middle age. She also worries there is a scarcity of quality men for her to meet as many are already in partnership or otherwise uninteresting. She also believes that her commitment to Simon obligates her to exhaust every resource (reading self-help books, talking with him, and going to couples and individual therapy) to try and fix the glaring issues within their relationship before she gives herself permission to leave. Joanna also likely has some shallow Unworthy Groove tendencies, believing herself less than deserving of a man secure enough to be comfortable with her many successes, the existence of her past lovers, and her inner and outer beauty that continue to attract male attention.

In the process of healing from her time with Simon, Joanna is sad, but also beautifully kind and understanding with her tender self. She doesn't berate herself for ignoring the initial signs that activated her intuition in the beginning. She is grateful for all the wonderful times she and Simon shared and the many useful lessons she learned, including noticing when potential partners may exhibit insecure behaviors indicating they may be overly mired in the Inadequacy Groove.

Perhaps most important, Joanna gains data about her own inner guidance, learning that her intuition is a valuable source of trustworthy information that was available from the very beginning of her relating with Simon.

Moving forward, her decisions for intimate partnerships include a stronger reliance upon her guidance which she listens to sooner, spending much less time gathering additional data from potential partners. Joanna is not sorry for her time with Simon; rather she is grateful the experience taught her that her initial instincts can be trusted, and she recognizes more quickly when her own fears of scarcity and other behaviors stemming from Unproductive Grooves try to falsely steer her choices.

People living within their Guidance Groove choose to cultivate circumstances and opportunities for connection with their guidance. Research indicates that participating in activities such as exercise or meditation can intrinsically increase happiness. These activities may also be those which increase your ability to access the guidance that informs your decision-making process and allow for greater connection with your own intuition. For me, access to my guidance increases with movement like walking, rowing on my backyard ergometer, bicycling, or by doing something I love which requires little thought, like cooking, baking or listening to specific music. Find and then cultivate whatever helps you tune in with and hone a connection to your guidance.

When you are on the Guidance Groove path, you reject those influences that can lead to choices out of alignment with your authenticity. You practice behaviors to align your choices with your own guidance. You root your decisions within an intentionality for the best and highest good. You protect yourself from the onslaughts of life that feed the false stories arising within the four Unproductive Grooves. You develop strong and positive self-talk messages to rebuff the negative chatter created by the fear motivators driving the four Unproductive Grooves.

When stuck in one of the four Unproductive Grooves, you choose to let situations in life reinforce, deepen, and sustain false stories underlying your grooves. Instead of recognizing life's circumstances as a series of opportunities to choose connection with guidance and authenticity before acting, you view life events as building blocks for your counterfeit stories. This view of life reduces your power and further separates you from your own guidance and authenticity.

The relief that you experience when you follow your Guidance Groove stems from an unwavering adherence to your own authenticity. Following your intuitive guidance provides you with autonomy and the ability to flow freely with life's circumstances. You can choose, at every juncture, to maintain alignment with your own authenticity. This autonomy reinforces your liberation and freedom and manifests as happiness, peace, contentment, and ease.

Living by the tenets outlined in the Guidance Groove is a learning experience and the journey will require your most sincere self-inquiry, study, perseverance, and daily practice to become easily accessible and automatic. Be extra kind and patient with yourself as you progress because escaping from a well-honed Unproductive Groove can be tricky and initially uncomfortable. Your process of advancing and regressing as you learn, practice, and experiment with living according to your guidance may not be in a constant positive trajectory. That's OK because there are no mistakes—throughout this process, you are collecting data and discovering how best to live more in alignment with your own guidance.

To track your progress and encourage your continuation, keep a journal or use the notes pages at the end of this book and describe what your guidance and intuition are telling you regarding choices you face every day. Take notes on how your choices unfold to gather data confirming or refuting your initial choices arising from guidance. If you prefer, use a sketchbook to draw your intuitions and outcomes. Use these notes and sketches to refine your connections to your guidance and learn to better discover and trust your intuitive guidance.

The Ravine: An Allegory for Escaping Unproductive Grooves

Imagine you're stuck at the bottom of a ravine. It's not terrible in your ravine and you have adequate food, water, and shelter. You even enjoy the scenery and company some of the time, and the flashfloods that occasionally swamp the ravine and threaten to undo your life are only periodic, not constant, and they are frequently predictable.

But something shifts. The flashfloods increase, reducing your periods of relative comfort. Food is harder to find, and your shelter keeps getting disrupted. The ravine is all you know, so you struggle harder to rebuild the hut that keeps washing away. You try, but increasingly fail, to find comfort, ease, and contentment.

At some level, you have always known that you must leave this ravine. And, with the increased discomforts you're experiencing, it's clearer than ever that you must leave to find deeper, more consistent comfort, support, and ease. Your instincts have always told you that, at the top of the ravine, there is sunshine, blue sky, less hardship, more ease, more resources, and a deep, steady comfort that is lacking in the familiar, but ever-darkening, ravine. You also strongly suspect that, at the top, the flashfloods don't pool and crash and destroy as they do within your ravine.

As circumstances in the ravine deteriorate more, you seriously consider leaving. Those around you don't want you to go as they've grown used to your presence in the ravine. Your presence helps justify and buoy their own existence in the ravine. They whisper that it's dangerous up top, unknown, and if you try to leave, the comfortable familiarity of the ravine will call you back down anyway. It may be a

31

mess with constant flashfloods and the resulting instability, but it's your ravine and it's known, so it feels safer than the unknown of the top.

Finally, the discomfort is so strong, that you follow the call of your guidance and start to climb out. The walls are slippery with mud, but, with practice, you soon discover that small indents hide beneath the mud, perfect to support reaching hands and climbing feet. You learn to find these and hold on. You talk to yourself as you climb, silently encouraging your progress, cheering your victories, and forgiving your slips back down. You discover others want to also leave the ravine and feel brave enough to try. When you work together, you make more progress, encouraging each other, reaching to provide support between the footholds, helping fend off those who try and pull you back down.

You reach the top many times, only to slip and fall partway back into the ravine. The going is difficult and demands so much of your attention. But each fall is smaller and smaller, each escape to the surface quicker, lasting longer. With each moment you spend on the surface, you gather data. There is sunshine and blue sky. There is rain, but it doesn't flood your home, it simply wets the outside and provides fuel for growth. Those who helped you out of the ravine become your steady confidants, your cheerleaders, your friends, and you find an intimate partner who shares your desire to be free of the ravine.

You have less and less contact with those who stayed in the ravine because you discover they no longer feel comfortable, friendly, or safe. They don't support your new life outside of the ravine. You may mourn their loss, but the relief at being out of the ravine and the deep knowledge that you are serving your best and highest good ameliorates the mourning.

You've written it all down as you've progressed so you can be reminded that your intuition was right. You can look back at your path and take encouragement from the distance you've traveled.

As your guidance long ago predicted, it is better at the top of the ravine. And you have the courage and perseverance to get there and remain.

I have lived through many circumstances wherein I followed my guidance even when it didn't make sense on the surface, or it felt uncomfortable because it wasn't what I "should have" been doing. Yet, the outcomes turned out better than I could ever have imagined. I collect these stories from my own experiences, and I use them to remind myself that when I trust my guidance, I experience outcomes most in alignment with the best and highest good for all involved.

Learning to Trust Your Guidance: Quitting a Great Job

It is the late 1990s and I am sitting at my desk in Seattle, my home city, at a job I love as a Research Scientist at NOAA's Marine Mammal Lab. I have a master's degree, and my job is challenging, fun, safe, and secure. Logically, there is little reason for me to quit what is essentially my ideal job and go back to school for a doctorate. I don't need another degree to continue in a positive trajectory with my position. I am living in the city I love with my family nearby, and I have a great boyfriend and a wonderful group of supportive, loving, and very fun friends.

But even with all this goodness, something nags at me. It is an insistent whisper of guidance. If I want to expand my areas of research beyond those mandated by my position and gain more autonomy to pursue other scientific interests, then I need a doctorate degree. I need to leave my NOAA job and become an academic at a university.

Underlying all of that is a deep instinct telling me that, if I ever have children, an academic position could provide the greater autonomy and freedom to plan my time so I could be most present as a parent.

I don't want children. As a field biologist, I spend far too much time away from home gathering ecological data in far flung locations to accommodate a child. Plus, kids are uninteresting, and I believe they would only hold me back from what I really love—my work, friends, boyfriends, and the rest of what makes up my life.

All that to say, it makes no logical sense to quit my job to go back to school for an advanced degree I don't think I need for job satisfaction and to provide greater future freedom to raise kids that I don't plan to have.

But that voice, that guidance, that instinct, won't leave me alone.

When I share my decision to leave and go back to school, I meet some resistance, but not much. My boss and co-workers are supportive, my friends and family are sad to see me move, but happy for my new trajectory. It is a relatively gentle push with lots of support, but still feels mournful and it's a challenge to push myself out of my comfort zone, move away from my beloved friends, family, and relatively happy life in Seattle, and join a difficult and lengthy doctoral degree program at the University of California, Santa Cruz.

But the relief I experience when I initially make the decision is enormous and that outweighs the grief and hardship. The deep knowledge that I am on the right path helps me continue and keeps guiding me forward.

In Santa Cruz, I meet Christian and we marry. I give birth to our son in the last year of my degree, and I earn a fellowship that allows me to spend time writing my dissertation for publication while also being present for my son. I get a post-doctoral position with no field work for two years after that, then I am hired as an Assistant Professor at UC San Diego where I can choose to do field work or not. I can even choose to bring my husband and son with me on my field trips—and I do, many times.

Everything my intuition whispered (with increasing urgency) about leaving my great job in Seattle was true. Even though it all seemed illogical at the time, I did need the extra degree to obtain a job with more freedom and more autonomy with my time so that I could be most present with our son. And although it took many years for me to see the full fruition of my choices, the positive outcomes I experienced because of my decision became strong data points supporting my growing thesis that it is absolutely essential for me to trust my guidance.

The processes for aligning with your Guidance Groove are meant to be used often, for every decision, so opportunities for practice are constant. If an outcome feels wrong, just try again. Take a longer pause, feel deeper, correct, refine, and you will find your authentic path forward. Make the decision arising from your guidance, take the action to move forward on your authentic path, then recognize and extricate yourself from whichever Unproductive Grooves are misleading you.

I understand living by the blueprint of the Guidance Groove may not be comfortable at first. I recognize access to guidance from your source may be difficult to find. Regular adherence to your Guidance Groove takes commitment and practice, which could make it seem like drudgery.

However, when you view each opportunity for living within your Guidance Groove as a potentially exciting, interesting, and fascinating surprise, then any sense of drudgery vanishes, leaving only the joy of exploration. I approach every single choice with curiosity. I ask, with a wondering openness, "What will my guidance lead me to decide? What will the outcome look and feel like? What unusual experience will arise that I may never have considered before?" There is a fresh and welcome freedom in not knowing exactly what will happen until your guidance provides you with a nudge. You may end up heading off in directions that were entirely unexpected. Allow for that surprise, welcome it, and delight in the gifts of the unknown.

Finally, I am certain everyone can connect to their source of guidance. Connection to guidance requires resting in your present moment, calming yourself sufficiently to notice what your body is telling you, feeling the inclination that arises and encourages you to choose that which inspires absolute ease and alignment with your most real and unvarnished self. Then you act according to that inclination.

These concepts of quieting the mind and tuning in to your feeling body for best access to guidance are universal and ancient, underscoring my certainty that everyone can find, connect to, and act from their own personal source of guidance. For example, Joseph Campbell, the American scholar of mythology, said, "But I do know what bliss is: that deep sense of being present, of doing what you absolutely must do to be yourself." Other examples abound. In her song, Long Time Sun, Grammy nominated performer Snatum Kaur sings "May the pure light within you guide your way home." These ideas even saturate popular entertainment from characters in Star Wars urging each other to follow "the Force" to one of the sisters in Frozen II encouraging herself to make choices based on the inner voice that whispers her correct path forward. When you know to look, you see examples everywhere.

In addition, mindfulness, a tool rooted in Buddhism, teaches that freedom from suffering requires clear awareness of every moment, a tuning in to what is real and present, without the murk of believing false stories. Sam Harris, neuroscientist, best-selling author, and spiritual atheist says meditation is "…simply the ability to stop suffering in many of the usual ways…" and he describes the positive outcomes derived from the experience of meditation as "…an enormous difference between being hostage to one's thoughts and being freely and nonjudgmentally aware of life in the present. To make this shift is to interrupt the processes of rumination and reactivity that often keep us so desperately at odds with ourselves and with other people."

As the above examples demonstrate, the underlying concepts that allow for cultivation of and adherence to your own Guidance Groove are described repeatedly and across a multitude of sources, including popular culture, spiritual texts, inspirational writings, poetry, and TED Talks. Therefore, I'm completely convinced guidance is real and everyone can connect with their own guidance.

Many of you already know your guidance exists, you know you can listen to it, and you understand that you are happier when you allow yourselves to listen to and trust that guidance. Now, choose to live every moment within your Guidance Groove. Share your experiences with those who are just learning or who haven't yet learned to trust their guidance. The data you have already gathered to support your experiences with this process will be valuable encouragement for those who are less familiar with living according to their Guidance Groove.

You can identify and escape from your Unproductive Grooves, make adherence to your own Guidance Groove common practice in your everyday life, and feel the contentment, ease, joy, and wonder that results. And so can everyone else. Make it your goal, as it is mine, for everyone to experience the bliss of dancing to their own Guidance Groove. Take a moment to imagine what human relating would be like if everyone were allowed, encouraged, and supported to become more and more in tune with the music of their Guidance Groove.

The more you adhere to your Guidance Groove, the more living outside of your guidance will be intolerable.

The first step is willingness. Are you willing to set benevolent intentionality with every decision? Are you willing to recognize, then step out of your Unproductive Grooves, to wait, be present, notice your vast, endless, and very accessible guidance? Will you pause to feel with your whole body and mind for the intuitive guidance stemming from your source? And most important, are you willing to act on whatever guidance demonstrates as your most authentic path forward?

Will you choose to live within your Guidance Groove?

Are you ready to be authentic? Free? Joyful?

Yes. You are ready.

PART 2

The Unproductive Grooves

Habitually conditioned to avoid fear and insecurity,
most people compulsively cling to what is familiar,
even if it is very painful and confusing.

Adyashanti, spiritual teacher

For ease of navigation, the material within the chapters for Part 2 are presented in the following pattern:

Fear Motivator: Fear underlies, motivates, builds, and sustains each Unproductive Groove. All behaviors related to each groove stem from these basic fears. The Unproductive Grooves wouldn't exist without these fears, so they are presented first.

Unproductive Groove Definition: A brief description of that which creates and sustains each Unproductive Groove and general characteristics you exhibit when you adhere to a particular Unproductive Groove.

Ego Component: Each Unproductive Groove has an ego component. This refers to the additional difficulty of recognizing when your ego, or your sense of self-importance, contributes to your motivation to remain adhered to Unproductive Grooves. You know your ego is playing a role in maintaining your Unproductive Groove patterns when you think that stepping outside of your grooves will result in you "looking bad" or "being wrong" and your ego will be diminished. To avoid taking what you perceive would be a potentially painful hit to your ego, you choose to remain stuck in your Unproductive Grooves. You'd rather be inauthentic and perceived as "special," then authentic and genuinely joyful. Once you release your attachment to the ego component, escape from the Unproductive Grooves becomes easier.

Self-talk: These are the messages you repeat to yourself inside your head when you are stuck in an Unproductive Groove. These messages, which are usually not true, work to keep you believing that you must remain entrenched in your groove.

Recognition: These are brief descriptions of general behaviors associated with each Unproductive Groove to help you recognize how your patterns may or may not fit with a particular groove.

Manifestations of the Unproductive Grooves in the Life Arenas: Short examples of behaviors arising from each Unproductive Groove that span the five life arenas described in Chapter 2.

Examples: Here I give deeper examples that label and define behavior types that exemplify elements of each Unproductive Groove. These are designed to help you recognize how adherence to an Unproductive Groove can lead to false identities and beliefs that drive multiple aspects of how you relate to others and that prevent authenticity, ease, contentment, and joy.

Initial Steps to Quit: Each chapter ends with the initial steps that will help you let go of living within that chapter's Unproductive Groove.

Deeper Examples for Leaving Unproductive Grooves: These parts delve more into the specifics required for some of the behavior types to break free of behaviors aligned with the Unproductive Grooves.

As you move through the next four chapters in Part II, I invite you to look at yourself in the most sincere, fearless, and vulnerable ways so you can best identify your Unproductive Grooves. Then you can apply the principles of the Guidance Groove to your own choices for more authenticity and freedom.

Once you understand the ways in which you adhere to Unproductive Grooves, you'll notice how others around you do the same. Their well-being might also be improved when they can recognize the futility of their grooves. Invite your loved ones to join you in their own liberation journey. However, please do not use this book to push others to change in the hope their transformation will improve your life. Dancing freely to one's own Guidance Groove can only be successful if each human makes their own conscious choice to do it.

CHAPTER 3

The Inadequacy Groove

Fear Motivator: You are afraid you lack the skills required for success and that others will discover your deficiencies and judge you negatively.

The Inadequacy Groove is created and sustained when you believe you don't have the adequate skills to be successful at whatever task is before you. You believe you are not good enough for what may be required. You compare yourself to others and feel you don't measure up. When you adhere to the Inadequacy Groove, you are insecure and terrified your inadequacies will be on display. You constantly try to cover up or deflect attention from your perceived inadequacies which is ultimately exhausting.

When you are afraid your perceived imperfections will be exposed, you make choices out of alignment with your true guidance hoping to hide your perceived inadequacies. You take jobs that are too easy. You stay in relationships well after it is time to move on. You pressure your children to be what they're not in order to calm your own fears of inadequacy. You compare yourself against external factors and, when you fall short, you are overly harsh on yourself (and others).

Ego component: Your ego, or self-worth, is very connected to maintaining a false image of perfection so others don't find out you're less than everyone else. You think you should have the perfect job by a certain age, or you should have the ideal family or a perfect marriage.

If you haven't achieved these "shoulds," you fear it's because you are inadequate and not as good as others, and your ego hates that others may perceive you in this way.

Allen: The Creation and Deepening of an Inadequacy Groove

Allen is always the least coordinated kid in school and the most likely to be teased because he wears glasses and prefers quiet reading and solo outdoor exploration over the raucous sports games, group bicycle rides, and other activities enjoyed by his siblings and the neighborhood kids. His family doesn't understand his lack of interest in their passions, and they pressure him to be more like them. His dad repeatedly tries to engage Allen in various sports, and he inadvertently shames Allen over his poor attempts and lack of innate skills. Allen's feelings of inadequacy take root early, deepening with time as he continues to fail at the activities most prized by his family.

To combat feelings of inadequacy in group sports, Allen buries himself in schoolwork and solo long-distance running. He believes if he displays mastery of something, then his parents and siblings will finally recognize his worth, take him seriously, and praise him for his excellence, even if his expertise is related to topics in which they have little interest. This strategy doesn't seem to work when Allen is young, but, as he moves into adulthood, Allen continues to pursue his parents' approval by attempting perfection in his studies and running.

Allen earns a Ph.D. and becomes an outstanding biochemist. He contributes many notable research articles to his field, garners multiple grants, and designs experiments to answer questions of larger importance to society. He also runs marathons, embracing a regimented training schedule. He is very controlling with his time and pursuits, and when he fails to achieve a goal at work or runs a slower than expected race, Allen works harder and castigates himself for his perceived imperfections. He is harsh with himself, and his expectations of others are equally rigid, ruthless, and exacting. Despite Allen's seeming professional and fitness successes, nothing he does is ever enough to garner what he perceives as adequate recognition from his family or colleagues. In return, Allen disdains his professional relationships and speaks of other scientists' work with scorn. He cannot retain graduate students and post-doctoral researchers in his lab for more than a year at a time because he bullies them and castigates their smallest mistakes in order to draw attention away from his own perceived short-comings. He is still productive, but without the support of his colleagues and long-term consistency with his research team, he must do more of the work and finds himself frustrated at his lack of progress.

Allen's fear of exposing his perceived inadequacies prevents him from recognizing, valuing, and feeling gratitude for his many successes. Allen is deep within the Inadequacy Groove.

Self-talk Examples of the Inadequacy Groove

"I'm not as good as those around me."

"I'm not smart or educated enough."

"I'm not beautiful enough."

"If I'm not perfect, my inadequacies will be exposed."

"My success is never enough."

"I can't fail because the shame I'll feel when others discover my failure will be too great."

"I have to hide my inadequacies at all costs."

"I'm so stupid/lazy/bad/weak that nobody will ever love me."

"I never get anything right."

"I can blame others if anyone notices my failures."

Do You Recognize Yourself in the Inadequacy Groove?

You seek control of situations because loss of control means potential exposure of your perceived inadequacies.

You are highly critical of yourself and, when that's too painful, you criticize those around you to maintain a focus on others' faults so yours can stay hidden.

You blame others for your own unhappiness, while embracing the role of "victim."

You reject others before they have a chance to reject you because their rejection could reveal your inadequacies.

You avoid any appearance of vulnerability, creating a veneer of perfection to hide your inadequacies.

You strive for perfection, but nothing you achieve is ever enough because your belief in your own inadequacy is seemingly endless.

Manifestations of the Inadequacy Groove in the Life Arenas

School/Work/Life-path

You seek rigid control of your environment.

You take on tasks for which you are unprepared in order to appear more experienced than you are, but then you are terrified of failing, so you create diversionary situations to draw attention away from your lack of expertise.

You take on all proposed challenges regardless of your abilities, then frequently bluster your way through them for fear that a more moderate approach will be perceived by others as a personal failure.

You never admit you made a mistake, took on too much, are feeling overwhelmed, or in any way let others glimpse your feelings of vulnerability, doubt, or anything that may imply you are anything less than completely capable to complete the tasks before you.

You blame others when things go wrong.

You are passive aggressive or overtly aggressive with colleagues.

You are a bully.

Family

Parent to Child

You pressure your children for perfection.

You are domineering, controlling, blaming, shaming, and bullying when interacting with your children.

You act and speak in ways that teach your children to believe in the Inadequacy Groove, creating another generation mired in a false belief.

Grown Child to Parent

You try to please and impress your parents.

You brag or exaggerate to your parents.

You sneak around and lie to your parents to avoid exposure of your own inadequacies.

You greatly fear disappointing your parents.

You choose to align with your natal family over your own children and/or spouse.

Siblings

You compete with your siblings.

You brag or exaggerate your accomplishments to your siblings.

You reject and are mean and cold with your siblings.

You feel jealousy and envy toward your siblings.

You participate in back-stabbing behaviors to undermine your siblings.

Close Intimate Relationship

You blame, shame, bully, and are critical of your intimate partner.

You embrace the role of the victim in relation to your intimate partner (if only they were different/better, then I would be different/better).

You avoid intimate relationships thinking if you reject everyone first, then nobody will discover your inadequacies.

You engage in conquering behavior, pursuing sexual conquests without a desire for loving connection because true connection means becoming vulnerable to discovery of your perceived inadequacies.

Friendship

You brag and exaggerate your role in the stories you relate to friends.

You focus on yourself in conversations, complaining about others, embracing your perceived victimhood, and/or aggrandizing yourself to hide your perceived inadequacies.

Community

You openly or secretly scorn those in your community, gossiping about and denigrating neighbors, fellow citizens, and any other humans you encounter in your day-to-day life.

You put others down so you can feel elevated in comparison.

Examples

If you are stuck in the Inadequacy Groove in any of the life arenas, your behaviors may reflect some of those in the shorter suggestions above. To better understand how you may be stuck, here are some deeper examples.

Bullies use threats, intimidation, and violence in attempts to force others to do their will. You belittle, castigate, criticize, dominate, and control those around you. You make unreasonable demands, then are harsh and demeaning when those demands are unmet. The bullying behavior allows you to constantly shift attention away from your own perceived inadequacies and place the focus on the inadequacies of others. The bully behavior can manifest in any of the life arenas. Bullies exist on playgrounds, and in boardrooms, intimate relationships, and your own home.

Allen: Inadequacy Masked by Bullying

When Allen feels his academic position and stature are threatened because his students and post docs aren't producing to his level of expectation, he becomes a bully, threatening, castigating, and humiliating those who work in his lab. He blames them for any shortfalls in productivity and he demands excessive efforts to improve. Finally, Allen is essentially fired when he is denied tenure at his prestigious university, not because he isn't smart, productive, and earns ample grant money, but because nobody can work with him. His fear of exposing his long-ago created and nurtured beliefs in his own inadequacy spur him to continue bullying, for he cannot understand any other way to achieve what he perceives is vital to his well-being and continued existence.

Allen's record of fundraising and long list of publications is more than sufficient for him to obtain an academic position at another university, but he is hired under the condition that he has only two years to display a continuation of his strong academic track record to earn tenure. He is momentarily mollified, leaving his first position in a huff of blaming and shaming others. Soon, with the stress of seeming inadequate rising, the patterns of bullying emerge in his new position, and two of his graduate students quit within 6 months. This time, the fear of losing his job and never gaining tenure at a prestigious university, which is a pinnacle of success for an academic, starts to overcome Allen's fear of exposing his perceived inadequacies. Something must change or else Allen will fail spectacularly, revealing all his perceived inadequacies, and that feels like death to Allen.

Dramaticists generate or encourage external conflict and drama. You are surrounded by small and large melodramas, your life a picture of seemingly endless chaos, crisis, instability, and flux. Peace, order, and natural flow are in short supply, with little time for reflection and quiet or thoughtful interaction with yourself and others. You may be perpetually unaware of time, creating tension and anxiety with every late arrival. You encourage discord and gossip among others. You invite disorder and stress by taking on more than is realistic to complete a task, then complain about your busy and overscheduled life. You may wait until the last moment to finish a required project, then lament at the resulting upheaval and stress. Behaviors creating drama deflect attention outward, toward the external spectacle of the moment and away from any of your perceived personal inadequacies.

Loners hide perceived inadequacies by avoiding deep connection with others. You may have friends but avoid intimate partnerships. Or you seek lovers, but rarely make it to a first date or past the early dating phase. Social interactions feel awkward, and you replay conversations or situations, castigating yourself for saying the wrong thing. Your social awkwardness in interactions with others feels perpetually larger than life, convincing you everyone must have noticed your enormous inadequacies. To avoid these feelings, you reject potential love interests or friends before budding relationships have any chance of reaching a level where your vulnerabilities could be witnessed.

Perfectionists "gild the lily" on every personal endeavor. You spend too much time on work or schoolwork, convincing yourself perfect "gilded" products will hide the myriad ways in which you think you are inadequate. You bully yourself with endless critiques of your perceived shortcomings and strive to eradicate all imperfection. Your attempts at flawlessness may seem like a good thing, but going far beyond what is required for excellence often enables the perfectionist to ignore other responsibilities, joys, creative thinking, and life events because you feel uneasy if your time is spent on anything other than creating a veneer of "perfect" outcomes. The unease comes from a suspicion that anything less than perfection will expose your own perceived shortcomings. Your world is a narrow focus of creating and maintaining a façade of faultless outcomes and exteriors to the detriment of fully embracing the complicated nature of real life. You also push your perfection tendencies on those whose appearance and actions could reflect well or poorly on you, including your co-workers, family members, intimate partners, and friends.

Victims blame others for life's unhappiness or failures. You constantly blame external forces, such as other people, your parents, or chance events, for your current or past non-ideal circumstances. The constant act of blaming others allows you to deflect attention from your own perceived inadequacies and place focus on others. When you align yourself with the role of victim, you give up the responsibility for your own happiness. You abdicate all power to choose otherwise.

There are true victims, of course. Terrible things happen to people who are real victims of life's circumstances. I am not talking about that.

You have likely noticed a pattern in these examples. All involve behaviors designed to draw attention away from the possibility that anyone, including yourself, might detect your perceived inadequacies. If you are stuck in the Inadequacy Groove, discovery of your faults feels like death, and behaviors dedicated to preventing or avoiding that discovery paralyze you into a negative feedback loop.

Initial Steps to Quit the Inadequacy Groove

To free yourself from the Inadequacy Groove, you must first recognize when your behaviors are emblematic of this groove. Review the examples above. Realize every behavior related to this Unproductive Groove is a choice. When you feel compelled to be highly self-critical, blame others, bully, complain, exaggerate, or in any way act to cover the fears of revealing your perceived inadequacies, *stop*.

Recognize the choice in front of you.

Set your objective to choose an outcome rooted in benevolent intentionality.

Notice every thought and comment as a choice to remain stuck in the Inadequacy Groove or follow your own Guidance Groove. You make the decision to be critical of yourself, or not; critical of others, or not.

Ask yourself:

"Do I need to take action (go for a walk, meditate, etc.) so I can better find, hear, feel into, and connect with my inner guidance?"

"What purpose is served by my self-criticism?"

"What am I trying to deflect by complaining about a situation or person?"

"Am I blaming others for negative circumstances so I can avoid taking on any blame or responsibility for my own actions?"

"Does embracing the role of victim allow me to avoid responsibility for my unhappiness instead of making active choices to support my happiness?"

"Am I critical and controlling of my children because I'm afraid if they're not perfect, my inadequacies will be exposed?"

"What is my internal guidance telling me?"

"What choices can I make to serve the best and highest good?"

Choose to be vulnerable. Come out of hiding and reveal your truest nature first to yourself. Notice the world doesn't end. Turn inward and notice how changing your internal dialogue into one seeking true guidance relaxes the reflexive urge to remain stuck in the behaviors and patterns emblematic of the Inadequacy Groove.

Continue to practice sincere vulnerability with yourself and then expand to reveal more and more of yourself to those whom you deeply trust. Notice how you are received. Explain you are stuck in a groove, it is not real, and you need to practice choosing to act differently so you can disengage from the false stories that keep you adhered to the Inadequacy Groove. If you are unable to explain this to a trusted person, explain it patiently and kindly to yourself. Imagine your most valued loved-one coming to you with this concern, this desire to change a destructive pattern, then treat yourself as you would that loved-one. Treat yourself with love, acceptance, curiosity, patience, encouragement, and care. Practice deep understanding and empathy with yourself as it may take time and a good deal of practice to disengage and instinctively tap into your authentic guidance rather than return repeatedly to your old, untrue stories of inadequacy.

Deeper Examples that Show How to Leave the Inadequacy Groove

Let's return to the previous examples to better understand practical ways to notice the choices before you, connect with your truest guidance, then act from authenticity, not fear. As you read the next part, keep in mind these examples are "flavors" or aspects of behaviors that manifest from beliefs inherent to the Inadequacy Groove. While the exact labels (bully, victim, etc.) are different, the flavors or essence of the behaviors are similar and thus connected.

The Bully in the School / Work / Life-path Life Arena.

As a bully, imagine how differently your interactions would manifest if you recognized you are simply afraid your co-workers or boss or subordinates might find out how completely inadequate you are for the job you hold. Of course, this is very likely not true, and simply stems from the patterns of the Inadequacy Groove, but you, the bully, believe your inadequacies are absolutely true.

If you, the bully, do something wrong at work, your initial Inadequacy Groove-inspired response is to blame, shame, and point fingers at others to draw attention away from your own perceived or real short-comings.

Instead of falling into this automatic response, *stop*. Take a deep breath. Recognize the opportunity to *choose* a different reaction. What action would serve the best and highest good? For you? For the company? Your co-workers? What does your guidance recommend?

Likely, the best good for everyone involved is for you, the bully, to recognize your part in whatever went wrong. Or recognize nothing did go wrong, but the instinct for bullying behavior came from the fear something would go wrong and you would be blamed. You feared your inadequacies would be on display to everyone at work. You would be shamed, humiliated, and everyone would know you are a fraud.

Recognize these feelings. *Empathize* with the part of you that feels them. Hold that part of you with these deeply ingrained Inadequacy Groove fears in a metaphorical loving embrace and assure that part of you that it is OK. The fears arising from the Inadequacy Groove are not real.

Discover you have a choice before you. A choice to act differently.

Once you recognize the destructive self-talk in which you bully yourself or take actions to bully others, then you can say to yourself, this happened because I made a mistake or I was afraid of making a mistake or I was actively trying to avoid any appearance of my own inadequacy. You can then feel into your source of intuition and guidance. Hopefully, you have taken time to figure out what situations work best to find and feel into your guidance. Maybe you need to take a break, go for a walk, sit quietly, or listen to music. Do that. Take a moment or ten.

Once in touch with your guidance, you will know the course of action most in line with your true authentic self. *Choose to take that path.*

If you make a true mistake at work, perhaps it is most in line with your guidance to immediately own it. Reach out to whomever may have been hurt or bothered or inconvenienced. Tell them your part and invite them to work with you to reach a satisfactory resolution. Be strong, resolute, simple, and honest. Resist the urge to overly blame yourself or others. Simply own it, fix it, learn, and move on. Perhaps you haven't made any mistakes, but you are in constant fear your potential for error will be discovered, so you bully all around you. In this case, seeking understanding and empathy from your co-workers can help break down this misconception. Sharing your fears invites a warm light to shrink the fears until they are manageable or non-existent.

Allen: Asking for Help to Stop Bullying

Facing another potential job loss due to his compulsion to bully his subordinates to distract himself and others from discovering his perceived inadequacies, Allen becomes increasingly uncomfortable and desperate. When the discomfort is too strong, Allen throws caution to the wind, and shares his fears of not making tenure at his new university with Greg, a friend he's known since college. Allen acknowledges his bullying behaviors but blames the students for their stupidity and laziness.

Greg loves Allen, and he recognizes Allen's brilliance and his capacity to contribute good to the world with his excellent work. But Greg has also repeatedly witnessed Allen's futile efforts to avoid professional failure with his harsh treatment of Allen himself and of those who work for Allen. Greg realizes that, in asking for help, Allen's fears of being fired have become stronger than the fears his bullying bluster is trying to hide. Greg is kind and rises to the occasion, offering to be a sounding board for Allen during those times when Allen's fears of failing become too much. Greg also encourages deep introspection by Allen, inviting him to try and connect with whatever is driving Allen's need to bully those with whom he works. He also urges Allen to find a good therapist to discuss these tendencies. Perhaps if he better understood why he acted this way, he could stop.

Greg is one of the few people Allen trusts completely and their shared history and affection make it safe for Allen to take Greg's words to heart. On his long runs, instead of castigating himself for his supposed failures, Allen starts to quiet his mind. He feels into the terrible fears of inadequacy that he has repeatedly tried to ignore with his drive for professional and fitness success. Allen remembers feeling small and dismissed by his parents and siblings for not conforming to their idea of what it meant to be a successful child and young adult. He feels into the shame he experienced when he felt their disappointment and the armor of control he built to defend his young vulnerability. In a moment of clear insight, he feels what it must be like for his students when he castigates their efforts because he felt the same impotence and inadequacy as a child. This insight is a turning point for Allen, and he shares his newfound empathy for himself and his students with Greg who praises and encourages Allen's progress.

Allen practices feeling into his place of truth every day during his runs, in the shower, on his commute, and whenever he has moments free to quietly reflect. He finds a therapist who feels safe and makes regular appointments. He learns what it feels like when his fears of failure arise and he talks to himself with kindness, empathizing with the child inside who can sometimes still feel so small. He talks with the technicians and students working in his lab, revealing that he really wants to achieve tenure, but he can't do it alone and needs their help. He explains that his perfectionist tendencies are meant to maintain an illusion of control to help lessen his fears of being exposed as inadequate. He apologizes for his bullying behavior and, when he feels a pull toward intimidation behaviors, Allen steps away from a situation, and asks for time to consider whatever has come up. Over time, the fear of inadequacy fades and he is more and more capable of feeling into his guidance for clarity on handling situations at work. He is no longer ruled by the fear of appearing inadequate in front of others.

Allen achieves tenure at his second university and is more successful in his mid-career than he ever was in his earlier days. Even more important, now that Allen is not constantly wasting emotional and mental energy on the frantic drive to hide his perceived inadequacies with bullying, he experiences a greater overall peace, clarity, and ease. This increases his ability to connect with his guidance and he applies it to more and more aspects of his life, sustaining the positive feedback loop of the Guidance Groove.

The Perfectionist in the Parent to Child Family Arena

As a perfectionist, you cannot bear to present anything but a flawless family façade to your friends, extended family, and whomever may observe you, your partner, or your children. You also actively avoid facing and dealing with any potential discomforts that arise within your family, preferring to believe in a false front of perfection even to yourself. By pretending you and your family are living a perfect life, you can avoid facing any fears associated with your own false feelings of inadequacy as a parent, spouse, and person.

You post frequently on social media, but you only share carefully staged and touched up photos with everyone in your family seeming happy, well-groomed, and harmoniously engaged in whatever fun activity is portrayed. You rarely or never share you or your family members' doubts, shortcomings, challenges, or worries, even with yourself, your spouse, your children or your parents, siblings, and closest friends. When others relate their typical marital, relationship, or child-rearing problems, you may show exaggerated or genuine empathy, but you also make a concerted effort to smugly assert that you and your family members don't experience such issues.

You project a false front of superiority, but you are secretly terrified that if anyone should find out that your child is less than brilliant or your marriage is a struggle or everyone bickers during family outings or you let your children play video games on their own for hours at a time because you're busy with work or just need time alone, they will think you are a terrible parent and partner and that feels like a full condemnation of you as a person.

It's exhausting for you to constantly maintain an appearance of excellence as it requires shopping for and buying the exact right clothes, creating the appearance of exceptional situations in which you force your family to pose and repose for photos that are up to your standards, and haranguing everyone to look and act within the narrow confines of what you deem sufficiently impeccable. You obsessively ruminate on past scenarios of you and your family's interactions with others, castigating yourself, your children, and your partner for behaving in ways that reflect poorly on your family and, by extension, you. You continually police the behavior and appearance of your spouse and children lest they inadvertently reveal your family's real or imagined insufficiencies, and you become furious and demanding when they don't live up to your unrealistic expectations and standards. That leads to perpetual unhappiness, disconnection, and secretive behaviors because everyone in the family is afraid of your wrath should they present any authentic, complicated, unhappy, or otherwise seemingly unsatisfactory parts of themselves to you or the outside world.

Now, imagine if you could fully understand that nobody worth having in your life cares about your perfection. Nobody is judging you based upon the perceived achievements and flawless appearance of you and your family. And, if they are judging you based on those shallow metrics, then they are not the people you want to have in your life as friends and loved ones.

You alone are creating this torment of such a narrowly prescribed existence. You are choosing to constrain yourself and your family within a box of phony excellence. Your fears of being exposed as inadequate are causing you to act in unreasonably demanding ways that are undermining opportunities for authenticity, connection, love, openness, and genuine support among the members of your family.

This includes refusing to face, discuss, and otherwise acknowledge actions and behaviors by you and your family members that don't conform to your view of perfection. You refuse to even talk about uncomfortable topics that reveal the normal and complicated nature of relating authentically among humans because to do so would mean you are admitting to the existence of your own and your family's potential inadequacies.

The next time something occurs that threatens to expose you and your family as the typical, messy, and complicated collection of beautiful humans you are, and you feel the urge to correct, run from, or otherwise act in ways to hide these perceived flaws, *stop*. Take a deep breath. Recognize the opportunity to *choose* a different reaction. What action would serve the best and highest good? For you? For your partner, your children, and your family as a whole? What does your guidance recommend?

Perhaps it's best to simply let go and observe the flow of life that occurs during and after whatever action is happening that may imperil the veneer of perfection you constantly strive to maintain. What do you see, feel, experience? Are you or your family members scorned or ridiculed? If you are with people who truly care about you and your family, then they will treat you and the situation with understanding, kindness, and possibly even complete disinterest because they are too busy happily living their own lives to care about any perceived inadequacies in your family. Perhaps they welcome the display of authenticity in your family's moment of truth. Observing the normal reality of life within other families helps remove or reduce barriers to connection that can exist when everyone is busy pretending that everything is perfect.

Once you start to realize that the insincere presentation of the perfect family is not necessary for you to receive validation, love, and recognition, then you can let go of more and more of your unrealistic expectations. Instead of ignoring, hiding, or running away from mistakes, chaos, altercations, and other potential "flaws" that arise within your family dynamic, embrace these uncomfortable circumstances for what they offer. These situations are golden opportunities to explore more deeply with your family members the causes of certain behaviors and they are invitations to navigate the discomfort together. The byproducts of encountering, accepting, and navigating discomfort together with true, honest, and open sincerity include greater personal growth and understanding and deeper and more meaningful connections with your partner and children.

When you insist on hiding behind a false front, you prevent others, including your children and your partner, from deeply knowing you. You also perpetuate hiding behaviors within your family and with everyone around you. That contributes to increasing inauthenticity, disconnection, and unhappiness for everyone.

By bravely facing and working to understand factors leading to dysfunction in your family, rather than pretending they don't exist, you allow yourself and everyone within your family to be more open, honest, and sincere in their relating with you. Further, when you share your challenges with those outside of your family, they may feel less alone in their own normal familial struggles. In this way, you are contributing to their own efforts to come out of hiding and increase their authenticity.

Living within your Guidance Groove is not about creating and maintaining a perfect life. It's about naturally moving with the flow of life and embracing whatever arises from a place of wholeness, guidance, and love, not fear. For a perfectionist, this can be extremely uncomfortable at first. You are used to trying desperately to control your family and their appearance to others. Dive into that discomfort. See what happens. Are you harmed? Are you belittled? Or are you welcomed and is your bond with your family members stronger after the discomfort of delving into the untidiness has passed?

Practice consistently facing, moving toward, and embracing imperfect messiness. Learn to look for and welcome those "messy" invitations to forge deeper bonds with your loved ones. Start small and notice what happens. Build on those small advances, write down or otherwise take note of how you feel as you increasingly release your beliefs that your adequacy is predicated upon you and your family's false pretense of perfection. Listen to your sincere guidance rather than the false story that your worth is dependent upon seeming perfect to yourself, your family, and the outside world.

The Victim in the Close Intimate Relationship Life Arena

Remember, when you enact victim behaviors arising from the fear motivator driving the Inadequacy Groove, you are *not* a true victim. Instead, you choose to blame others for your discontent, you choose to align yourself with a victim mentality in order to push the focus outward and away from your real or perceived inadequacies. True victims have had something terrible happen to them beyond their control and their circumstances do not apply here.

To align yourself with a victim mentality means to give up all your power to be authentic, free, liberated, content, and happy. Deciding the actions, behaviors, and feelings of others are responsible for your happiness, contentment, and ease means you cannot affect freedom for yourself. Imagine if you recognized your contentment and happiness are not dependent upon anyone else but only you. *Only you.*

If you feel perpetually unhappy in your close intimate relationships, you, the victim, are certain it is because your partner doesn't contribute enough to the household, is never home, not affectionate, messy, unintelligent, unsexy, overworked, lazy, mean, boring, weak, rude, preoccupied with the children, etc. You complain about their perceived inadequacies and lament how much better your life would be if only they or the circumstances they created were different.

Your discontent manifests by nagging them to change or haranguing them about past events in which you perceive you were victimized. You strongly believe your own happiness and contentment could be achieved if your love partner transformed themselves into a better person or made different choices.

You, the victim, thus have dual roles. First, you must badger your love partner, pester them, and wear them down with constant suggestions for improvement in the hopes they will finally see the error of their ways, change their behavior(s), and stop ruining your happiness.

Your second role is to complain about your own perceived victimhood—to anyone who will listen. You mourn the loss of your own opportunities because your love partner forced their will on the relationship, preventing you from: finishing school, taking a great job, having children, or otherwise realizing your perceived potential. You have abdicated all accountability for your own shortfalls, missteps, and unwise choices. Everything negative in your life can be attributed to the inadequacies of your love partner.

Now, imagine you alone are in charge of realizing your potential. You alone can create situations in which to foster your own peace, freedom, and contentment.

Feel the power in that realization. You are *not* a victim of your close intimate partner. You are a willing participant in the path you have co-created with this person and you can change your part of it. You cannot change them or their part or their path. Only yours.

You alone can make the choices to realize your own liberation. You can choose to reject the behaviors of the false victim. You can face yourself, admit your discontent, recognize your accountability, then choose the steps toward living in your Guidance Groove.

Recognizing the futility and wasted time of spending so much energy blaming your love partner for your unhappiness can be devastating. The fear of exposing your own inadequacies by accepting responsibility for your own happiness can feel enormous. However, you will feel a deep relief when you truly understand your choices alone lead to your own happiness or discontent. You have the power to choose. Only you.

As you process this great sadness and relief, empathize with yourself and your love partner. Hold yourself and your partner in a space of love and forgiveness. Share your revelations with them and fully admit your own part in your current situation. Invite them to join you in rejecting your role as a victim. Share your fears and allow them to see your vulnerability. Perhaps you both can forge a way forward together or perhaps you can reach an amicable dissolution. Regardless of the outcome of the intimate relationship, you can choose new behaviors in alignment with the Guidance Groove.

In Conclusion

All behaviors arising from the Inadequacy Groove are designed to shift attention away from your own perceived inadequacies. Thus, the examples, though providing a narrower focus, can be expanded and applied to any aspect of the Inadequacy Groove. If your Inadequacy Groove tendencies don't exactly fit within the life arenas depicted in the deeper examples, then please, take some time to think about, write down, and clarify how your Inadequacy Groove behaviors manifest. Perhaps picture a famous person, a fictional character, or someone you know who fits one of the deeper examples of the Inadequacy Groove. That may help as you navigate your own way out of a different aspect of the Inadequacy Groove.

Further steps for releasing from the Inadequacy Groove, and the other Unproductive Grooves, are detailed in Chapter 7.

CHAPTER 4

The Obligation Groove

Fear Motivator: You are afraid you will be labeled selfish and irrelevant unless you remain committed to fulfilling false obligations.

The Obligation Groove is created and sustained when you believe your own well-being should be sacrificed rather than risk disappointing, hurting, or in any way letting down those around you. You set your intent to please others rather than listening to your own guidance. You don't want to experience the repercussions of upsetting the status quo or feel guilt for choosing what is best for you.

These tendencies lead you to hold onto obligations long past what is necessary. You also believe that if you release tasks and let others demonstrate competence, you will no longer be relevant or needed. You will become dispensable and replaceable. So, you take on more commitments than necessary, to the detriment of your own authentic desires and goals.

There are a range of experiences within the Obligation Groove—from people depending upon you overly much because you consistently take on too many tasks out of obligation (the People Pleaser) to you becoming overbearing in your desire to foist your services on those who don't need or want them in order to create a sense of your irreplaceability (the Martyr).

When you allow yourself to be bound to others and to situations from a sense of obligation, rather than from alignment with the best and highest good, you waste time and foster anger, resentment, sadness, and unfulfillment within yourself and others. You make choices out of alignment with your true guidance and authenticity. For example, you stay with intimate partners despite a deep knowing the relationship is long over. You unnecessarily postpone your own career or education or other life goals to care for family members, children, or spouses. You sacrifice hobbies, fitness, and time with loved ones to clock extra-long hours at work. You spend time with caustic "friends" instead of choosing only to surround yourself with those who nourish and support you. You take on extra tasks because you are afraid to say no. You allow your fear of feeling unnecessarily guilty hold you in unproductive situations.

When you are stuck in the Obligation Groove, you also use your perceived commitments as excuses to hide from fulfilling your own potential and to ignore your intuition and guidance. Like some in the Inadequacy Groove, you blame external factors (perceived obligations) for your own inaction, inertia, unhappiness, and unfulfillment. Blaming external forces allows you to reject responsibility for your own unhappiness or stagnant life situations.

Everyone chooses true obligations that are important to fulfill, such as the obligation to feed, house, and otherwise care for your children, the obligation to perform a job well to create success, and the collective obligation to be kind and loving toward others. These obligations are different from those created when you are trapped in the Obligation Groove.

Rely on your growing discernment to tell the difference between responsibilities to which you have committed that are in alignment with your best and highest good and those which are created by you to keep you tethered in the Obligation Groove. This chapter will help you make those delineations.

Ego component:. Your egoic self-worth depends on thinking only your talents are useful for the company or work project, only you can properly care for your children and other loved ones, your intimate partners will be crushed to find you no longer love them, or only you can successfully organize the school event. You fear that, unless you continually try to do it all, someone better will replace you and you will be needed for nothing. To be unneeded feels like death. You use your heightened sense of obligation to elevate yourself above others as you think you alone are capable of completing a certain task in an acceptable way. The fleeting sensations of superiority and false assurance of indispensability are more alluring than the experience of calm, connection, peace, and authenticity available when you learn to step out of the Obligation Groove and make choices more in alignment with your guidance.

Rachel: A Commitment to the Obligation Groove

Rachel is outstanding at organization, and she thrives in her job running a large, successful business. She also loves control and feels she is without direction or purpose unless she maintains laser focus on her job and managing her life, the lives of her husband and two grown daughters, and, to a lesser extent, the lives of her extended family, friends, and employees. She feels obligated and compelled to direct those close to her and she is convinced their lives, or her business, will crumble if she isn't constantly overseeing everyone's endeavors. She revels in how her family and employees constantly look to her for direction and she refuses offers from others to take over some of her more menial tasks. Her daughters are in their late-20's, Shelley is married and working as a human resources manager at a large company and Christine is single and a popular high school math teacher.

When Rachel's husband leaves her to pursue other romantic relationships after 30 years of marriage, Rachel is secretly devastated and mortified that her carefully constructed life has fallen apart so spectacularly. She convinces herself that she needs to work harder to fulfill her perceived obligations as everyone's caregiver and she assures herself that, despite her husband choosing to leave her, the supervisory role she plays in the lives of others ensures that she is worthwhile. Thus, Rachel doubles down on her job, and her micromanaging tendencies spread from her daughters to her siblings, parents, nieces, and nephews. She sends out reminders and task assignments for Christmas dinner at least a week before Thanksgiving. She spends days leading up to Thanksgiving organizing, cooking, and arranging the extended family gathering held for the first time at her married daughter Shelley's home.

Her family appreciates some aspects of the manifestations of Rachel's Obligation Groove behaviors. There is always a nice, beautifully decorated, and outwardly successful celebration during all the important holidays. But it usually comes with stress-inducing and overly aggressive demands from Rachel in the weeks leading up to the event. Everyone is told what to bring, how to dress, and where and when to show up. The menus, themes, and times are all dictated by Rachel, making it easy for nobody else to do a thing. When others don't agree with her ideas or plans, they are steamrolled and shamed into compliance by Rachel's refusal to let anyone else have any semblance of control and by her complaints that she is under appreciated for all she does for the family.

Despite the seeming ease of having to contribute very little to every family gathering because they all know Rachel will handle the details, all members of the family feel various levels of exasperation, resentment, and fatigue when faced with another missive from Rachel as to how any upcoming family event will unfold. Rachel's daughter Shelley and her husband wish they could be allowed to plan and execute

Thanksgiving dinner at their home according to their own desires, without interference from Rachel. They try to decline Rachel's many offers for help, but she continues to push herself into every detail and she ignores her daughter with somewhat patronizing and belittling comments ("Oh darling, you'll never be able to organize a full turkey dinner for all 24 of us! It'll be a lot of extra work for me, especially as I'm in the busy season at work, but I'll handle it.") as Rachel pushes herself into every detail. Eventually, they give up trying to get their way and vow to travel to Mexico on their own next year to avoid Rachel's overbearing demands. Rachel is deep within the Obligation Groove.

Self-talk Examples of the Obligation Groove:

"My loved ones need me and only I can fulfill that need."

"Nobody else can do a good enough job."

"My situation may not be ideal, but it's better than what's out there."

"Her/his/their feelings will be hurt if I do what's best for me."

"I promised to be there, so I must. Even though I hate it."

"If I let someone else do the work, then nobody will need me."

"I hate feeling guilty, so I better say yes even when it's not good for me."

Do You Recognize Yourself in the Obligation Groove?

You feel stuck in your current situation because you made a commitment to stay.

You don't change circumstances that are uncomfortable or wrong because you are afraid of the unknown and you also fear potential negative repercussions if you upset the status quo.

You frequently take on tasks above and beyond what is required for a successful outcome.

You never have time for yourself, your recreational pursuits, or people with whom you really want to connect.

You embrace the role of martyr, sacrificing your time, needs, wants, and goals in the name of fulfilling your duties to work, family, community, or others.

You neglect to pursue and cultivate your own truly desired education or career goals, instead using your obligations as excuses to do nothing.

You refuse to leave or modify your close intimate relationship because you are afraid of hurting the other person and/or are afraid to face the unknown on your own without a partner.

You don't express your own needs for fear they will be ridiculed and dismissed as selfish, and you'll be bullied into continuing to meet the needs of others.

You believe changing your current situation will prove too painful or inconvenient for others, so you do nothing.

You believe only you are competent enough to successfully complete certain tasks.

You feel guilty when contemplating saying no to any request.

You fear if you say no, people will stop asking, choose someone else, and you will become irrelevant.

Manifestations of the Obligation Groove in the Life Arenas

School/Work/Life-path

You work longer hours than necessary.

You micromanage projects, forcing yourself into every aspect to control every detail so you will seem indispensable.

You take on extra work and volunteer for tasks that are in addition to your core job.

You remain in jobs long after your skills are beyond what is required.

You maintain the status quo in all realms, fearing anything new will diminish your obligations and your perceived worth.

You take on all household and childcare duties, so they'll be "done right," but then you complain when nobody helps you.

You ignore your true dreams, desires, and goals as you help others achieve theirs.

Family

Parent to Child

You refuse to deny your children's requests.

You place your children's needs (however minor) above your own.

You always volunteer to help at your children's school.

You refuse outside help to care for your children in order to make time for your own pursuits.

You don't trust your co-parent and believe they are not as good as you at childrearing.

You feel selfish and unnecessarily guilty if you're not always available for your children.

You act and speak in ways that teach your children to believe in the Obligation Groove, creating another generation mired in a false belief.

Grown Child to Parent

You refuse to deny a parent's request.

You place your parents' needs above your own or your spouse's and children's needs.

You act as sole caregiver for an ailing parent, rejecting offers of help as you believe only you can provide the proper care.

You feel selfish and guilty when you say no to your parents.

Sibling

You feel resentment, envy, and anger toward siblings who are not as invested in parental caretaking or other parental-related tasks.

You feel jealousy and resentment when your non-obligated siblings are welcomed, loved, and praised by parents and other siblings even though they do little to help the natal family.

Close Intimate Relationship

You feel resentment and anger toward your live-in partner when they don't share household duties and childcare, while simultaneously refusing to request their help because of your unnecessary guilt, and the beliefs your partner won't do a good enough job or will discover they don't need you anymore.

You stay within your unhappy relationship out of unnecessary obligation-related feelings of guilt, fear of hurting your love partner or family, and/or fear of being unneeded and unwanted by anyone else.

Friendship

You allow harmful people to waste your time under the guise of friendship.

You choose to spend time with people out of obligation, even when there is nothing productive, nourishing, or positive in your interactions with them.

You do favors and otherwise overly extend yourself for demanding friends who take advantage of your tendencies to act from the Obligation Groove.

Community

You volunteer for tasks in your neighborhood, church, school, etc., that others won't do, even when they bring you zero joy or reward.

You perceive always volunteering increases your value to the community and allows you to feel superior to those who don't volunteer.

You block participation by others so your contributions, and potential value to your community, aren't diminished.

Examples

If you are stuck in the Obligation Groove in any of the life arenas, your behaviors may reflect some of those in the shorter suggestions above. To better understand how you may be stuck, here are some deeper examples.

Loyalists remain committed to a situation or person even when doing so is harmful, counter-productive, and out of alignment with true guidance. You persist with home situations or jobs or friendships or educational pursuits despite deep sensations of unease, unhappiness, turmoil, fear, dissatisfaction, discomfort, worry, and nervousness. You decide your commitment to something, or someone, is more important than your own ease, happiness, and well-being. You, the loyalist, believe if you made a promise, you must fulfill it, even if the promise was made in good faith, but has now been shown as a mistake. You are afraid you will feel guilty, and others will perceive you as selfish, shameful, unkind, and dispensable if you break your commitment. You believe your steadfast adherence to unproductive people and situations increases your significance, making you a "better person" than those who leave fruitless and ill-chosen circumstances to pursue their own true guidance

Martyrs create a veneer of value by becoming overburdened in fulfilling the needs of others. You perceive you are more valuable, significant, important, and needed because you alone can provide for those around you. You as a martyr complain loudly and often about your martyrdom so others will be aware of and compliment your sacrifices, further contributing to your façade of importance. You welcome that which makes you overburdened because you are then too busy doing something "valuable" for others to risk taking actions toward creating, owning, and living a life built on your own intrinsic value.

At first glance, the martyr may feel like a victim stuck in the Inadequacy Groove, but the motivations are quite different. Those in the Inadequacy Groove perceive they are victims of external circumstances to avoid taking responsibility for their own unhappiness. Martyrs willingly take on too much to both increase their value in the eyes of themselves and others and to avoid taking responsibility for creating their own happy lives. They choose to become overburdened as it then allows them to justify their demands for recognition, value, love, and time from others. Few people respond well to the martyr's demands for acknowledgment, leaving the martyr feeling more under-valued, unloved, unappreciated, and resentful. So, they complain more loudly and take on more tasks, thus perpetuating the cycle and increasing their unhappiness.

Rachel: The Martyr's Need to Control

Christmas is still three weeks away and Rachel complains to her sister and mother that nobody has responded to her emails regarding her assignments as to what to bring for the family dinner and to confirm their attendance. Her sister

Grace tries to explain that she isn't comfortable bringing dessert as she avoids processed sugar and doesn't make or eat sweets. Her mother Anne says that she would also rather bring something else besides the dish she was assigned as she has an idea for a new recipe she'd love to try. She also explains that she will be spending part of Christmas afternoon with her husband's family (Rachel's parents divorced when she was 8 years old) and is not sure she can get to Rachel's as early as Rachel would like. Rachel's response is to lash out with anger and hurt and she accuses her mother and sister of conspiring against her and not sufficiently appreciating all her efforts to create a perfect Christmas.

Instead of trying to mollify Rachel and rescind their comments, Grace and Anne surprise Rachel by refusing to give in to her demands. Her mother mentions that she is leaving her husband's family gathering early and she could just as easily stay there if it's too much trouble for Rachel. Grace shrugs and says she'd be just as happy with only stopping in for a glass of wine and offers to bring a couple of bottles for the family. Rachel panics. If nobody attends her choreographed Christmas dinner, or if they attend but bring only what they want to contribute, then not only will Christmas be ruined, but the obligation to her family that she has falsely created will become non-existent. Then she will have nothing to do, and nobody will need her. Those potential losses leave Rachel feeling empty, unmoored, unloved, and purposeless.

People-pleasers say yes to most requests from loved ones, colleagues, friends, and acquaintances, ignoring your own needs, wants, desires, and guidance. Your obligation to please others stems from your deep desire to avoid the potential for rejection or other unpleasant repercussions if you do anything that makes people disappointed, angry, or in any way unhappy with you. The people-pleaser is different from the martyr in that martyrs take on too much in order to feel valued by others, whereas people-pleasers say yes to all requests to avoid the potential for negative reactions by those who are asking for your service. You feel resentment toward people because their requests leave you constantly overextended, but your desire to avoid experiencing the upset of others is stronger than your desire to lead a balanced life.

There are two common threads for the people in these examples. One is the prevalence of behaviors dictated by a feeling of "should." You *should* sacrifice your personal well-being for your family/job/love partner/children because it is "right" or "good." To do otherwise would be "selfish" and "bad."

The second is the degree of self-value you perceive you are creating by remaining committed to your perceived obligations. To those of you stuck in the Obligation Groove, leaving perceived obligations feels as if you will lose this "value" and also be labeled a terrible person.

Initial Steps to Quit the Obligation Groove

To free yourself from the Obligation Groove, you must first recognize when your behaviors are emblematic of this groove. Review the examples above. Realize every behavior related to this groove is a choice. When you find yourself complaining about your excessive workload, making excuses for remaining in a destructive love relationship, avoiding your own needs to focus on those of others, or in any way acting to avoid feeling unnecessary or guilty or selfish, *stop*.

Recognize the choice in front of you.

Set your objective to choose an outcome rooted in benevolent intentionality.

Notice every thought and action as a choice to remain stuck in the

Obligation Groove or follow your own Guidance Groove. You make the decision to complain or not, wallow in unnecessary guilt or not.

You make the decisions to remain adhered to your perceived obligations or not. You decide to align with people and situations that nourish, protect, enliven, enrich, and expand your life. Or not.

Ask yourself:

"Do I need to take action (go for a walk, meditate, etc.) so I can better find, hear, feel into, and connect with my inner guidance?"

"What am I trying to avoid by choosing to remain committed to people, places, situations, and conditions long after they are unproductive, harmful, and dissatisfying?"

"Am I staying overcommitted to avoid discovering what I need to do on my own to be happy?"

"Do I choose to be overworked so others will deem me more valuable and deserving of their esteem and admiration?"

"Does embracing the role of martyr make me feel superior, needed, and indispensable?"

"What purpose is served by me staying within a discontented situation?"

"Am I afraid to stand alone, untethered to false obligations?"

"Do I have the capacity to be of genuine service to others right now, or am I needing instead to focus on the parts of my life that are truly important to me?"

"What is my internal guidance telling me?"

"What choices can I make to serve the best and highest good?"

Choose to set your benevolent boundaries. Alignment with your true guidance necessarily requires recognizing, setting, and holding personal boundaries. You are the primary guardian of your inner spark of radiance, your love light, your source of guidance. Without boundaries, your love light or source will become increasingly diminished so as to appear entirely lost. However, it is never lost. Never. It is simply starving and depleted from the behaviors arising from the Obligation Groove. Standing within your benevolent boundaries and guarding your love light with actions stemming from guidance and authenticity is *selfless*. Inviting your true source to guide your actions from your place of benevolent intentionality is the ultimate unselfish action. When you act from love and guidance, you can then easily help and serve others while standing firm in your benevolent boundaries without creating a poison cloud of false obligation.

You have the power to choose the people, events, activities, and work that are allowed access to your love light. Perceive what happens when you create and hold your boundaries. Escaping the Obligation Groove may require extra care and practice in setting and maintaining your boundaries as those around you may have grown accustomed to you surrendering your own needs, wants, and desires to fulfill theirs. Seek help from the people in your life who don't make constant demands on you. Bring them into your experience and share your desire to be more in alignment with your guidance instead of the behaviors associated with the Obligation Groove. They can help you understand that saying no to some requests is okay.

Reject the label of selfish. Others may call you "selfish." However, if you are making choices from within your benevolent boundaries, then you can recognize that this label is untrue. You may be reluctant to let go of the façade of importance you have created by letting others believe they constantly need you. Recognize these potential difficulties and empathize with yourself as you discover and learn to hold your love light protection boundaries.

Honor your autonomy. Practice expressing your independence in small ways. Notice the world doesn't end, literally or figuratively. Notice how you are received. Others may be surprised, put out, and try to pressure you back into obligation. If you are following benevolent guidance, stand firm and true. When you are free and autonomous, notice how your love light shines and grows. Then notice how your light diminishes when you meet the wants and needs of others in response to the fears driving the Obligation Groove. Your love light, which is your source of guidance, gets lost in a sea of "shoulds."

Practice recognizing when your input is truly not necessary. Observe what happens to your work or your family when you pull back and let others step in. Notice the physical sensation of releasing burdens with each subsequent "no" you express. Feel that relief. Notice your value is not diminished. In fact, there is great power in standing within your benevolent boundaries. Especially when your boundaries are firmly maintained with genuine kindness, care, empathy, love, and an honest and true commitment to the responsibilities that truly matter and bring you joy.

I am not suggesting you walk away from those who truly need you or shirk responsibilities at work or at home. I'm inviting you to follow the initial steps outlined in the first chapter so you can live within your Guidance Groove with every single opportunity to say yes or no to a request, commitment, or demand. You can then be of service to yourself and others from a position of genuine love and desire to help.

Deeper Examples that Show How to Leave the Obligation Groove

Let's return to the previous examples to better understand practical ways to notice the choices before you, connect with your truest guidance, then act from authenticity, not fear. As you read the next part, keep in mind these examples are "flavors," or aspects of behaviors that manifest from beliefs inherent to the Obligation Groove. While the exact labels (martyr, loyalist) are different, the flavors or essence of the behaviors are similar and thus connected.

The Loyalist in the Close Intimate Relationship Life Arena

You, the loyalist, ignore your guidance in the face of increasing unhappiness within your intimate relationship. You choose to stay partnered within the confines of the relationship out of misguided loyalty to others. You make excuses to tolerate the status quo of a non-vital, conflict-ridden, non-productive, unloving, unrewarding, or otherwise detrimental intimate relationship because you convince yourself leaving or changing your role in any way would be "bad." Bad for you as you will be alone and judged by others as selfish. Bad for your lover as their feelings will be hurt and they will feel rejected. Bad for your children if their parent is the one with whom you are unproductively linked because you feel obligated to provide them with an "intact family," regardless of how wrong the relationship has become.

Imagine a different scenario. Imagine approaching your lover from a place of open-hearted vulnerability, autonomy, curiosity, and absolute non-obligation or expectation. Imagine sharing uninhibited and spontaneous love, joy, passion, and other aspects of your true self with your lover. Without fear of obligating yourself or them. Each of you is fully free to experience joyful presence with the other. When it's time for engagement elsewhere, then you and your lover have autonomy and freedom to be fully present with the other people and other aspects of your lives. You have the autonomy to cultivate time alone, time to connect with your guidance, time to be your free self. Letting go of the loyalist behaviors increases your natural instincts to delight in, freely please, and effortlessly extend grace, love, and generosity toward your lover.

When you live by your own Guidance Groove, every single coming together with your lover is a mutual choice, a celebration sparked from autonomy, non-obligation, freedom, and genuine care, love, joy, and eagerness to connect. You recognize when your love connection is not driven by the best and highest good, then you take time to stop and rest into your intuition and highest self. You ask for guidance to discern which choices you can make to realign your connection with your intimate partner and bring it in balance with your best and highest truth. When you are on the Guidance Groove path with your lover, you both speak freely and with love to one another, inviting input from each other's wisdom and guidance. You choose to create a relationship of non-obligation together, providing autonomy, safety, love, and a promise of the freedom to always follow one's own intuition and guidance for every interaction. You come fully out of hiding from one another and build and rebuild your intimate relationship with a basis in truth, guidance, and mutual authenticity.

Sometimes the choice in service to the best and highest good requires ending the current iteration of your intimate connection. For the loyalist, ending a love relationship when it no longer serves the best and highest good can feel terribly selfish. Extenuating circumstances can accentuate those feelings of selfishness and disloyalty. Perhaps your lover depends upon you financially or you believe your children will be harmed if you leave their parent or your family/friends/religious community expect you to stay in your love relationship out of social or religious duty or you're afraid of hurting someone's feelings. These beliefs are uncomfortable. But the discomfort will be short-lived as you notice, recognize, welcome, and increasingly sink into the authentic relief, ease, and freedom tied to choosing outcomes serving the best and highest good.

To be clear, following your own guidance does not give you free rein or an excuse to harm your intimate partners or ignore the honest commitments and promises you made for their well-being. Pay careful attention to your actions. Feeling honest discomfort when we are truly selfish allows us to recognize when our actions are not in alignment with benevolent intentionality for the best and highest good.

Successful escape from the Obligation Groove for the loyalist requires you spend time cultivating connection to your true guidance to more easily understand when your actions are those of true selfishness versus those serving the best and highest good. Choosing to live in alignment with your intuition and guidance, then acting with benevolence and non-obligated responsibility toward those who will be disrupted by your choices will ultimately create freedom and ease for all involved.

The Martyr in the Parent to Child Family Life Arena

As a martyr, imagine how differently the interactions with your children would manifest if you recognized your Obligation Groove behaviors are attempts to garner value, validation, and love from your children (and potentially others). You, the martyr, are frequently unable to simply give or receive care, love, compassion, or help in a non-transactional way. It may seem as if you are doing way more than necessary for your children because you are selfless. There is no altruistic nobility in doing far more than necessary for your children to the detriment of living your own best life guided by your own authenticity. In fact, everyone's growing resentment and dissatisfaction clearly underscore the ignobility of your, the martyr's, choices. Your actions further exacerbate your false belief that overworking yourself for your children will eventually pay off in more love, acceptance, and validation from them. You perceive your overdoing for them allows you to make demands on your growing or adult children. You feel you deserve their value, love, and care because they owe it to you for all the extra work you do or have done for them.

If you, the martyr, feel undervalued in your role as a parent, your initial, Obligation Groove-inspired response is to do more for your children, complain about how much you do for them, then demand more from them in return. In the end, you are left feeling resentful and undervalued when you don't receive the acceptance, recognition, and love you seek from your children. The loop is endless and will never result in you, the martyr, receiving the validation and value you seek from your children because you are ignoring guidance from your highest self and acting from fear.

Instead of falling into this automatic response, *stop*. Take a deep breath. Recognize the opportunities to *choose* a different path. What action serves the best and highest good? For you? For your children? What does your guidance tell you?

The first step toward what is best for you and your children is to *recognize* when your behaviors stem from the Obligation Groove. *Empathize* with the part of you feeling undervalued, underloved, and underappreciated. Recognize when you unnecessarily insert yourself into situations, pushing your "help" on your children when it is not requested, welcomed, or needed. *Understand* your motivations stem from a fear that you will be deemed irrelevant, unlovable, and without value. Therefore, you force your "help" on your children to justify demanding their appreciation and love in return. Notice when the appreciation and love are not freely given by your children in response to your over-doing and pushing. Then notice if your fear escalates, driving you to do even more, complain even louder, and demand greater gratitude, admiration, and approval from your children. All of which become increasingly scarce as everyone's resentment grows.

Discover you have a choice before you. A choice to act differently.

Once you recognize your tendencies to garner value and approval by forcing your unneeded and extreme "help" on your children, you can change your self-talk messages. Instead of questioning your value and attempting to extort love and appreciation from your children by overdoing for them, you can value yourself for simply being yourself. You can then feel into your source of intuition and guidance. Hopefully, you have taken time to recognize and cultivate the activities and situations allowing you to find, feel, and connect with your guidance most easily. Instead of forcing yourself on, and making demands from, your children, take a break, go for a walk, sit quietly, reach for a trusted friend, anything that helps to break your Obligation Groove cycle and connect with your true guidance.

Once in touch with your guidance, you will know the course of action most in line with your true authentic self. *Choose to take that path.*

Resist the urge to impose your unrequested opinion, feedback, or "help" on your children (or anyone else with whom you experience the behaviors of the Obligation Groove). Learn to recognize how it feels to act from guidance alone and not from the fear of becoming irrelevant and unneeded. With every situation, every interaction with your children, stop, ask, "What action can I take or what choice can I make that will serve the best and highest good? What is most in alignment with my intuition and guidance?" If you can't find the answer immediately, then do nothing while you allow yourself time to connect with your intuition.

There are many ways you can be of authentic service to your children. First, when you feel the urge to provide help, care, and/or advice, pause to connect with your intuition. What is your guidance telling you? Can you be of service to your children without contamination from the fears driving the Obligation Groove behaviors? Are you clearly anchored within your benevolent boundaries as you freely nurture and support your children? Can you ask your children the ways in which help from you would be welcome without the expectation of anything in return from them? Can you release desire to interfere if they decline your offers of help?

Perhaps authentic service to your children involves nothing outward and no tangible outcomes. Perhaps simply holding them in a metaphorical loving embrace serves the best and highest good. Cultivating connections to your intuition, then tuning into your intuition for guidance every single time you want to be of genuine service to your children will help you break free of the martyr behavior patterns.

Once you decide the martyr behaviors are no longer aligned with your best and highest good, you may feel resistance from your children.

They are accustomed to receiving too much "help" from you and, while they may resent it and wish to be left alone to listen to and follow their own authentic guidance, they have grown dependent on your interference. Thus, they haven't learned to disengage and act according to their own true guidance with full responsibility for creating their own best lives. They may take advantage of your tendency to overdo and encourage your continued "help" despite the larger discontent it creates for everyone involved. They may be suddenly shocked when you no longer overdo for them and they may pressure you to keep overdoing for them, even though transactional giving driven from the fears of the Obligation Groove is contaminated and detrimental.

Be alert for this and resist the temptation to continue co-creating the increasingly deep trench of the Obligation Groove with your children. Talk with them about your own non-productive belief in the Obligation Groove behaviors, admit your false martyrdom, and explain your newfound goals to set and stand firm within your benevolent boundaries. Explain your intention to act with guidance from your intuition, to act from love instead of fear. Explain that you are new at this, and you would appreciate their grace, care, and patience as you figure out how best to interact with them in ways that are free of the Obligation Groove.

If they are not in a place to hear your explanations, then simply keep making your choices from benevolent intentionality. The relief and freedom you feel as you increasingly disconnect from the poisonous transactional love loop emblematic of the martyr's Obligation Groove will naturally extend to your children.

Rachel: Recognizing and Rejecting Martyrdom

Rachel complains to her married daughter Shelley that Aunt Grace and Grandma are rudely unappreciative and refusing to go along with her demands for Christmas dinner.

Shelley feels a sudden burst of support for and courage from the brave actions of her aunt and grandmother, so she shares that she and her husband will be out of the country for next Thanksgiving as the pressure of having the perfect family event was too much when they hosted the holiday a few weeks previous. Rachel is nearly apoplectic, but Shelley doesn't back down. It helps that her mother's interference in their Thanksgiving dinner caused strife between her and her husband because it led Shelley to realize her commitment to a harmonious marital union was more important than mollifying her mother's demands.

When Rachel complains to her other daughter Christine about everyone's lack of gratitude, Christine gently points out that Rachel's overly aggressive demands coupled with her martyred complaints do not serve to make others eager to spend their Christmas evening at her house. Rachel has heard similar comments many times before, but this time, she is able to listen. Perhaps it is the chilling prospect of becoming unimportant and unneeded as everyone drifts away to pursue their own holiday plans. Whatever the reason, Rachel finally begins to understand that her martyrdom and insistence on fulfilling her every perceived obligation is ruining her relationships. She even manages to acknowledge these behaviors likely contributed to her husband finally quitting their marriage to find happiness elsewhere.

Rachel takes a huge step and sends out a family email rescinding the food assignments and carefully scheduled timetable she had created for Christmas dinner. She instead offers to hold an open house for the family throughout the afternoon and early evening of Christmas. She describes the dishes she will contribute and invites everyone to bring something delicious to share that inspires them. Rachel feels genuine fear that nobody will come and there will be an absence of the right kinds of food. She has a moment of panic before she forces herself to send the email.

Over the coming days, the responses to her email are positive and she feels herself wanting to take over again, to ensure the evening is exactly picture perfect, but she pauses, remembers her family's feedback, and she lets it go. Christmas arrives and the open house is somewhat messy, with too many cracker and cheese plates and not enough main dishes and everyone arriving at different times. But overall, it's a pleasurable day and she accomplishes something she hasn't done in years: because everyone arrived at staggered times, she was able to spend time one on one with the individuals in her family, rather than being inundated by everyone at once. These more intimate opportunities led to deeper conversations, sharing, and connection among her and her family members.

As the new year progresses, Rachel feels into her newfound freedom from obligation, especially during her daily yoga practice. It's very small at first, but Rachel discovers an increasing relief each time she's able to loosen or release her grasp on one perceived obligation at a time. She finds she enjoys feeling into and listening to her own internal guidance to determine what really requires her attention and what can safely be handed off to an employee or another family member, or simply let go altogether.

With each step away from artificial obligation, Rachel discovers that her self-worth does not diminish. In fact, she notices her employees and family members paying more attention to her input because her contributions seem more thoughtful, less demanding, and are fewer than her previous habitual onslaught of interference. Rachel notes all these changes in a book she keeps in her nightstand. It . helps to reinforce her progress and assuages her fears that she will become irrelevant unless she interferes in the lives of those around her. This practice increases her trust in the process of tapping into, listening to, and following her guidance to choose outcomes for the best and highest good and reinforces and sustains the positive feedback loop of the Guidance Groove.

In Conclusion

The behaviors arising from the Obligation Groove are driven by fears that others will perceive you as selfish if you follow your authentic guidance. You may also fear you will lose your value if you say no to the needs of others. Recognizing the myriad ways in which these fears can manifest as different aspects of the Obligation Groove will help you expand upon these examples with more personalized applications. If your experiences within the Obligation Groove are not exactly expressed in these examples, take time to think about, write down, and clarify how your Obligation Groove behaviors manifest. Perhaps picture someone you know, or a fictional character or famous person, who fits one of the deeper examples of the Obligation Groove. That may help as you navigate your own way out of another aspect of the Obligation Groove.

Further steps for releasing from the Obligation Groove, and the other Unproductive Grooves, are detailed in Chapter 7.

C H A P T E R   5

The Scarcity Groove

Fear Motivator: You are afraid vital resources will run out before your needs are met.

The **Scarcity Groove** is created and sustained when you believe there is a finite supply of a specific and important resource, such as love, money, power, recognition, time, intimate partners, or access to a good job, school, or neighborhood. You fear these resources will be unavailable to you, either through the actions of others or life's circumstances, thereby thwarting your desire to attain what you believe is needed for your ultimate fulfillment and happiness.

To avoid these fears, you attempt to control the resources you believe are scarce and you try to control others' access to those resources. You feel jealous, resentful, and angry when others appear to receive more. You believe life is a zero-sum game, meaning any gain by others results in an equal loss for you, the one stuck in the Scarcity Groove.

When you believe that resources are scarce, you make life choices based on a fear of missing out, rather than allowing and following guidance arising from your intuition. You allow your fears of scarcity to hold you in all number of fruitless and painful circumstances. For example, you choose to pursue a practical college degree, one seemingly more guaranteed to yield a financially rewarding career, rather than following your true passions, which may be more financially risky, but personally more fulfilling. You are possessive with your intimate partners, controlling their time and attention for fear their autonomy will reduce their interest in you. You unduly restrict, control, or push guilt onto your children for fear their love of others and outside pursuits will leave less love and time for you. You commit to intimate partners too soon, convinced they will leave if you don't force commitment and then nobody else will be interested in loving you.

You hide or hoard knowledge or assets in your job or schoolwork, believing cooperative connection will diminish your own personal rewards. You deceive your clients or cheat on school exams, justifying your sneaky behaviors by believing you are entitled to the reward of money, respect, or good grades, and if you don't fight for those rewards using any means possible, you will lose out to others who will use even worse deceptions. The sensation of victory is brief because there is always another situation or person to control or manage or deceive or bully lest you are prevented access to your share of whatever resource you have decided is in short supply.

As with other grooves, if you are mired in the Scarcity Groove, you reject personal responsibility for your own unhappiness. Instead, you externalize the blame, pushing it outward to demonize anyone you perceive is impeding access to your fair share of valuable resources.

Please note I am not talking about true scarcity. Financial and emotional poverty are real and there are many social and other causes for these situations of true scarcity. In contrast, those of you mired in the Scarcity Groove are frequently privileged, but your groove behaviors stem from your false beliefs that you lack resources when you are clearly surrounded by abundance.

Ego component: You believe your superiority should grant you special access to whichever resource feels scarce. You use this inflated self-worth to justify your actions that allow you to maintain your access to, and block others from, whichever resource feels scarce to you. You use your feelings of supremacy and entitlement to justify unproductive behaviors designed to prevent others from threatening whichever desired resource seems rare. You give little thought to the needs of others, and you believe that control over people is required to prevent a personal loss of money, love, power, prestige, or any other valuable element you believe is in short supply.

You think only you know what is best for those you love, so your attempts to control them are simply for their own good. You believe only you are capable of insuring access to and safeguarding your portion of potentially scarce resources, so you bully those whom you perceive may also have access.

Katie: Building a Scarcity Groove with Constant Craving

Katie dreams of a career in entertainment from an early age, both because she craves the spotlight and she thinks performers make lots of money. Katie is the oldest of 6 children. There is never any extra money or excess attention as everything is spread thin across two loving but overwhelmed parents working hard to keep the large family housed, fed, and cared for. Nobody goes hungry, but there is never enough of the "good" food—snacks, sweets, burgers, and pizza. Same with clothes and space—everyone has what they need, but there are no new, popular, or stylish clothes and beds and bedrooms are always shared. If Katie doesn't act immediately to get whatever is considered good when the rare opportunity arises, then she goes without.

As Katie moves into adulthood, she constantly creates schemes to take advantage of situations that could help her gain access to resources she perceives are scarce. In a college internship at a local TV station, she steals the books sent by publishers for review by the local hosts and sells them at the used bookstore. She uses the work vehicle to run personal errands. She justifies the occasional cheating on her college exams by convincing herself she is taking only what is due to her. Plus, she figures all the other kids are wealthy, so have more time to study instead of working to earn money as she must.

During her internship, Katie receives chances to help produce segments for television and she is occasionally on camera with small, local-interest stories. The program manager notices she is a natural performer and begins inviting her to do more pieces on camera. She builds her career from there, eventually hosting a local daily morning show. She is not satisfied with this, considering the local show to be too provincial, but at the same time, she is terrified that she will be let go if someone comes along who is more attractive, smarter, and more able to draw viewers. Despite her unhappiness, she keeps hosting the TV show because she is terrified to quit lest she find herself with nothing.

As a local celebrity, Katie is frequently hired to host charity functions, moderate political debates, and otherwise participate in events where she is in the relatively small spotlight of her city and state. Katie takes every one of these jobs that come her way and volunteers for more. She does this to combat the anxiety of losing her talk show host job to someone superior and to increase her chances that someone will notice her talents and elevate her to a better position. She is unable to turn these jobs down, even when they are exhausting, don't pay enough, and are increasingly unsatisfying. Katie is convinced if she says no, someone else will say yes and that person will reap the rewards from the experience (whatever they might be) and she will be left out.

Katie is afraid jobs in her field are scarce and she won't get her chance unless she fights for and accepts every opportunity. These fears prevent her from saying no to the jobs that aren't serving her goals and are exhausting her. She also can't see that her natural talents in front of a camera and interviewing people are outstanding, so she fails to recognize, value, and feel gratitude for her many successes. Katie is deep within the Scarcity Groove.

Self-talk Examples of the Scarcity Groove:

"I must have a high-paying job to earn enough money to be happy."

"If I don't get married soon, there won't be any quality people left."

"My lover won't have enough time and love for me if they spend too much of these limited resources on their other interests, friends, and family."

"If my best friend meets other friends, they won't have enough love or time for me."

"If I don't say yes to this less than desirable job, I will never be hired by anyone."

"I feel jealous when work colleagues do well because their success means I won't get the recognition I deserve."

"Others will take up all the resources, so I must prevent them from gaining access to those resources."

"If I don't hold tight to this person or experience or object, they or it will be taken away."

"If I'm not continually working to get ahead, then others who are working harder will surpass me and prevent me from my own success."

Do You Recognize Yourself in the Scarcity Groove?

You are frequently worried about money, food, love, and other resources running out before you get your share.

You strive to always earn more money, regardless of the toll this takes on your personal life and self-fulfillment.

You are terrified you won't have enough, so you must horde the resources you do have, not sharing with others, including those within your own family.

You frequently attempt to control the behaviors of those you love, preventing them from connecting with other people, convinced their love of others will diminish their capacity to love you.

You are emotionally needy to the point of irritating those around you, including your intimate partner, friends, and children.

You are convinced if you don't demand and actively take your share of money, attention, love, or other resources, you won't get what is rightfully yours.

You never have enough of whatever you are seeking, not enough money, prestige, attention, job security, love, friendship, sex, or devotion.

You are not satisfied when you attain certain resource goals you thought would make you happy, instead looking ahead to acquire and control more.

Manifestations of the Scarcity Groove in the Life Arenas

School/Work/Life-Path

You say yes to any and all offered jobs, projects, and invitations, for fear opportunities will dry up if you decline, and you'll be left irrelevant and without any future prospects, money, and/or friends.

You overextend yourself in multiple arenas so as not to miss potential opportunities and to prevent others from access to these opportunities for fear they will perform better than you, further diminishing your chances for future success.

You micromanage, dominate, and block involvement of others in projects or social engagements to prevent them from potentially outperforming you, because you believe accomplishments by others diminishes your chances for future success.

You sabotage perceived rivals and refuse to share your discoveries or collaborate within a team to protect your position or share of the credit.

You cheat or otherwise act without integrity to do well on performance metrics (exams, work reviews, etc.).

Family

Parent to Child

You whine, wheedle, demand, and use guilt or other negative methods to force your children to demonstrate love for you.

You complain your children don't spend enough time with you.

You jealously restrict your children's time with other family members, friends, or outside activities.

You hover, overprotect, overschedule, and practice "helicopter parenting," fearing if you allow freedom for your children, they will be harmed or inadequately prepared to achieve and guard their own resources.

You act and speak in ways that teach your children to believe in the Scarcity Groove, creating another generation mired in a false belief.

Grown Child to Parent

You assume your parents give more time, gifts, love, and other resources to your siblings and their families.

You consistently try to impress or draw attention from a withholding parent in hopes of receiving more of whichever emotional, financial, or other resource feels scarce to you.

Siblings

You try to outcompete your siblings, hoping to garner more affection and attention from your parents.

You experience jealousy and envy when your siblings do well.

You sabotage your siblings and speak ill of them to other family members so you will seem better.

You assume your siblings receive more parental attention than you.

Close Intimate Relationship

You act needy and clingy with love interests, always demanding more and attempting to control their behaviors to alleviate your abandonment anxiety.

You choose unsuitable partners, simply because they show interest, for fear nobody else will offer love.

You commit to a partner too quickly or rush intimacy for fear the other person will leave if they are not "locked down."

You manipulate love interests to try and get more from them than they offer.

Friendship

You complain when you perceive friends do not spend enough time with you.

You are needy and demand attention from others and pout or hold grievances when you perceive you're not receiving enough attention.

You feel jealous when friends talk about other friends or other pursuits outside of your friendship.

You pressure new friends for early and unearned closeness, afraid they will leave you before a true bond of friendship has time to develop.

Community

You remain aloof within your community, saving your scarce time and other resources for your immediate family and yourself.

You view others in your community with suspicion, convinced they will take advantage of you if given the chance.

You are convinced your home, possessions, family, and property require extraordinary security measures to keep others from gaining access to your resources.

Examples

If you are stuck in the Scarcity Groove in any of the life arenas, your behaviors may reflect some of those in the shorter suggestions above. To better understand how you may be stuck, here are some deeper examples.

Cheaters act without integrity across multiple life arenas. You falsely inflate your own performance or sabotage the performances of others to protect your own access to what you perceive is a scarce resource. You do this at work, in school, with friends, intimate partners, and in any situation in which you believe sabotage, lying, gossiping, and other underhanded behaviors are necessary to safeguard your own current and future resources and block others from "threatening" those resources. You believe others are also cheaters, thereby justifying your own unethical behaviors and further feeding your fears of scarcity.

Graspers anxiously cling to resources, be it friendships, intimate relationships, jobs, or opportunities, refusing to share or release any part of what is vital to survival. You are needy and your need is a bottomless hole that can never be filled, regardless of the accolades, friends, lovers, jobs, prestige, or money you accumulate. Your deep belief in scarcity prevents you from believing that your acquired security is real and lasting. As a grasper, your needs are so vast, and you are so mired in scarcity, that you don't believe any evidence that could convince you otherwise.

Micromanagers prevent others from experiencing full autonomy and freedom by always attempting to exert control over co-workers, lovers, friends, and family. You fear that allowing others full independence will diminish their reliance on you, the micromanager. You also fear that those around you will surpass and rise above you, garnering more of the already scarce resources, leaving you, the micromanager, behind. You may also believe that those you care for will lose out on accessing scarce resources if you don't constantly interfere to control and micromanage all situations.

Overschedulers take on too many jobs, projects, and plans with friends and loved ones. You fear that, if you say no, then you won't be asked again, and already scarce money, prestige, and/or relationship opportunities will diminish or disappear entirely. These same scarcity fears motivate parents who overschedule their children with multiple extra, "enrichment" activities. As a parent who is an overscheduler, you are afraid your children will be underprepared for challenging schoolwork or non-competitive for sports teams or elite universities, thereby further reducing your children's chances of attaining goals you perceive are available only to very few. You, the overscheduler, feel perpetually exhausted and unhappy with your busy life, often yearning for quiet time to connect meaningfully with your work, yourself, your children, other friends, and loved ones.

Some of the outcomes, such as too many commitments, experienced by overschedulers are similar to those experienced by the martyrs stuck within the Obligation Groove. However, the motivations are different. Martyrs take on too much to increase their perceived value and feed their egoic beliefs that only they are capable of whichever task is before them. Overschedulers are afraid to say no to any offers lest someone else take their place, thereby further diminishing the overscheduler's access to resources they already perceive to be scarce.

Katie: Overscheduling to Combat Fears of Scarcity

Despite her relative success as an entertainment journalist, Katie is constantly terrified it will all vanish unless she is constantly on her grind. Eventually, on a Sunday afternoon when Katie is rushing to a charity event for which she is hosting the fundraising auction, her despair at the difficulty of her overscheduled life reaches a fever pitch. She is exhausted because she was up late the night before interviewing a famous novelist on stage at a local theater and she spent Friday evening partying late with her friends and met a date for brunch Saturday morning. Her overscheduling tendencies stemming from her deep fear of missing out are most apparent in her work life arena, but it spills over into the social aspects of her life as well. She can't say no to invitations from her friends, accepts dates from men who aren't that interesting to her, and is always looking to make friends with people she perceives can help her advance her career goals. Katie is already dreading having to be up early Monday morning to prepare for and host her local TV show. She also needs to prepare for a meeting later in the week as an executive at the network for which her local station is an affiliate has approached her with the chance of creating and hosting segments as a regular correspondent on their daily, national mid-morning show.

Katie makes it through the Sunday evening event but is late to work Monday morning because she slept through her alarm. Her boss is concerned and asks if she is alright. Katie has been late to work more and more and her performance hosting her show has declined. Katie is so busy that she has less time to focus, prepare, and be entirely present for her

TV hosting job which pays most of her bills and provides a modicum of public recognition. Katie pushes through and focuses on her meeting later in the week with the network executive. The pressure to do well is enormous and entirely created by Katie's fears that one mistake will result in her losing everything–the spotlight, her earning potential, and any chance at becoming more famous. She is also convinced that, if only she were offered the network job, she could finally relax, be more secure, and she could quit some of the exhausting small-time gigs.

The day before her network interview, Katie is asked to fill in that evening to host a local charity event held annually by the wealthiest family in her city. Along with this family, Katie knows that many other rich and connected people from her state and elsewhere will be in the audience. The event is scheduled to end late. She also knows that her interview is scheduled for early the next morning as the network executives are in a time zone 3 hours ahead of hers. Katie feels strongly that taking this gig is a bad idea and she should instead focus on preparing for and being extra sharp and present for her morning interview. However, Katie cannot say no. What if she isn't offered the network job? She might need whatever connections she makes at the charity party to elevate her position. She accepts the job, stays to schmooze late in the evening, then dials up for her video conference interview feeling bleary, underprepared, and shaky from lack of sleep and drinking too much alcohol the night before. No amount of makeup hides the circles under her eyes. Something must change or Katie's overscheduling will cause her to lose this and every other opportunity and her beliefs in scarcity will all come true.

Initial Steps to Quit the Scarcity Groove

To free yourself from the Scarcity Groove, you must first recognize when your behaviors are emblematic of this groove. Review the examples above, feel into the behaviors that contribute to your unhappiness, and see if they fit within the Scarcity Groove. Realize every behavior related to this groove is a choice. When you find yourself or your children exhausted and stressed from too much activity, clinging to and micromanaging intimate partners, friends, children, and loved ones, cheating on an exam or work project, sabotaging others, or in any way acting from the fear that you will be denied access to what you perceive as a scarce resource, *stop*.

Recognize the choice in front of you.

Set your objective to choose an outcome rooted in benevolent intentionality.

Notice every thought and comment as a choice to remain stuck in the Scarcity Groove or follow your own Guidance Groove. You make the choice to grasp onto resources, control those around you, and believe there is not enough to fulfill your needs. Or not.

Ask yourself:

"Do I need to take action (go for a walk, meditate, etc.) so I can better find, hear, feel into, and connect with my inner guidance?"

"Am I hovering over, micromanaging, overcommitting, and overprotecting my children?"

"Am I afraid if I don't interfere, my loved ones won't stay safe and they will lack the skills needed to fully access and maintain the resources required for a "happy" life?"

"Am I always focused on the next achievement I think I need to reach instead of enjoying, feeling gratitude for, and appreciating my successes in the moment as they occur?"

"Do I demand too much from my friends, romantic partners, and family, clinging jealously, fearful I will lose their love if I don't control them?"

"Do I resist sharing money, food, recognition, knowledge, time with loved ones, or other resources for fear there won't be enough left for me?"

"Am I willing to cheat on an exam, sabotage a co-worker, or in any way diminish others to elevate myself if I perceive my performance will suffer in comparison to others if I don't take action?"

"When I'm asked to take on a task, job, project, or invited to a social event or asked on a date, do I say yes for fear I will never be asked again if I say no? Do I say yes because I really want to do what is asked or do I say yes because I'm afraid someone else will say yes, then they will outperform and eventually replace me?"

"What is my internal guidance telling me?"

"What choices can I make to serve the best and highest good?"

Choose to believe in abundance. Notice all the ways in which your life is full and overflowing with resources. Every instance of abundance in your life is an example which counteracts your unfounded beliefs in scarcity. Chronicle these examples so you can add to the list every time you recognize abundance in your life. You can return to this list when your scarcity fears arise. Feel the gratitude for all you have and all you were given on your path toward realizing your current abundance. Identify and acknowledge the tools you already possess that allow you further access to resources.

Recognize how previous experiences could foster a belief in scarcity. Perhaps you were raised in financial poverty, so now, as an adult, you deeply fear you or your children will lose access to money, food, housing, or other basic needs. Perhaps your parents or intimate partner are stingy with their distribution of love and affection, fueling your beliefs that love is finite and withheld unless you demand it and grasp onto the people you wish loved you more.

Empathize with yourself and extend an understanding and loving hand to that part of you whose basic human needs may not have been met at points in the past, thereby contributing to your current attachment to the Scarcity Groove.

Deeper Examples that Show How to Leave the Scarcity Groove

Let's return to the previous examples to better understand practical ways to notice the choices before you, connect with your true guidance, then act from authenticity, not fear. As you read the next part, keep in mind these examples are "flavors," or aspects, of behaviors that manifest from beliefs inherent to the Scarcity Groove. While the exact labels (grasper, cheater, overscheduler, micromanager) are different, the flavors or essence of the behaviors are all similar and thus connected.

The Grasper in the Close Intimate Relationship Life Arena

Graspers latch onto close intimate partners, attempting to control your lover's time, behavior, or activities. Your deep belief in the scarcity of love causes you to believe any time or attention your partner gives to others will result in a loss of love and availability for you. You, the grasper, are excessively needy, demanding more attention, love, sex, and time, then you complain to and criticize your lover when those needs aren't met.

However, because your emotional needs are endless, and you are so mired in your beliefs that support, love, and connection are scarce, or can be taken away at any minute, there is absolutely nothing your lover can do to convince you otherwise. No action or word from your intimate partner is enough to reassure you, the grasper, that you are truly loved, accepted, and safe within your relationship. Once your lovers realize their actions will never be enough to fill your endless neediness, they frequently leave you in exhaustion, thereby fulfilling your scarcity story, and exacerbating your needy behaviors with future intimate partners.

As a grasper, imagine how differently your interactions with your lover would be if you realized the demands you make stem from fears motivating the Scarcity Groove. Hounding your lover to fill you up will never work because you are too convinced there is a shortage of love available to you.

Imagine if you realized you alone can fulfill your own neediness.

If you, the grasper, feel panicked when your lover makes plans to do something fun without you, your initial Scarcity Groove-inspired response may be to cling onto your lover, complaining that they should be with you.

Instead of falling into this automatic response, *stop.* Take a deep breath. Recognize the opportunity to *choose* a different reaction. What action would serve the best and highest good? For you? For your lover? What does your guidance recommend?

The best good for everyone likely involves you acknowledging your fear of being left out or abandoned. You fear your lover will find others more interesting, stimulating, or fun than you, eventually choosing other people and activities to pursue, leaving you alone. You fear if you don't control your lover, then your endless needs for connection will never, ever be met.

Recognize these feelings. **Empathize** with that part of you that believes in the patterns inherent to the Scarcity Groove. Love that part of you and notice the ways in which a fear of scarcity may have arisen from past experiences and beliefs. Catalog the many ways in which you have abundance within your love relationship, so you have evidence that the fears arising from the Scarcity Groove are not real.

Discover you have a choice before you. A choice to act differently.

Once you recognize the ways in which you sabotage your close intimate relationship with unreasonable demands for your lover to fulfill your vast neediness, then you can choose to act differently. Tap into your guidance. Do the activities that most foster your connection with your guidance. Go for a walk, ride your bicycle, meditate quietly, listen to music, or commune with nature. Take your time and really feel into the situation before you. What serves the best and highest good when your Scarcity Groove fears arise? How does it feel to badger your lover for constant validation? What good is served when you unleash unreasonable demands on your lover?

Once in touch with your guidance, you will know the course of action most in line with your true authentic self. *Choose to take that path.*

Perhaps it is in alignment with your guidance to talk kindly with yourself and say, "I can love myself, I can nurture myself, I can be present for myself, and the needs I perceive to be vast can be fulfilled by my own love, honor, and commitment to myself. My lover does not have the responsibility to fulfill my needs or make me believe that my Scarcity Groove patterns are not real. It is by my own actions and choices that I can fill my own needs."

Talk with your lover, be vulnerable and express your acknowledgment of the needy behaviors arising from your Scarcity Groove fears. Come out of hiding and be simple, direct, and honest. Explain your behaviors arise from fears that are not real, but those fears, over time, have become ingrained as truth within you. Describe your desire to be more authentic, happy, and free by accessing your guidance to make decisions that serve the best and highest good, rather than acting from fear. Seeking empathy and camaraderie from your love partner in your desire to make choices in alignment with the Guidance Groove can enhance the love and light shining on your fears, further diminishing their power.

The Micromanager in the Parent to Child Family Life Arena

You, the micromanaging parent, feel the fears of the Scarcity Groove in relation to your children on two fronts. You are afraid your child will lack access to scarce resources, such as basic safety, acceptance to a good university, or access to the best teachers, sports teams, or social circles, if they are free to make their own choices. You also fear losing your child's love, a resource you perceive as limited, if they are allowed to love and depend upon others.

In your attempts to reduce those fears, you prevent your children from experiencing full autonomy and freedom. You micromanage your children at all stages, from the playground to college and beyond, interfering and interjecting yourself at any opportunity as you attempt to control all aspects of your child's life. You deny or discourage reasonable requests for exploration and new experiences, under the guise of protecting their health, safety, well-being, and status. You interfere with their friendship choices, classes, and extracurricular activities, intervening at any opportunity lest your child make a misstep that could result in your child losing out on whatever resource you perceive to be in short supply.

You, the micromanager, also believe the attention and love you receive from your children will diminish if they are allowed to experience unfettered love and connection with other people, even your child's other parent. You view love from your child as a finite resource which, if shared with others, will mean less love for you. Rather than recognizing that your overprotective behaviors stem from your beliefs in the Scarcity Groove, you justify your excessive hovering and interference because you, the micromanaging parent, believe your actions are necessary to both safeguard your children from the world and prevent them from depending upon or loving you less.

Instead of falling into this automatic response, stop. Take a deep breath. Recognize the opportunity to choose a different reaction. What action would serve the best and highest good? For you? For your children? What does your guidance recommend?

To begin, it is important to recognize that choosing to have children requires accepting that you are creating another human who is separate from you. You will not be present for every single moment, thought, action, and interaction your child experiences with the outer world and with their inner selves. Yes, the potential for disaster, heartbreak, and disappointment exists, as it does for all who live on Earth. However, challenging experiences presented by the natural flow of life are also invitations for increases in personal growth, introspection, and inner strength. To withhold these opportunities from your children by overly shielding them from life's tough experiences denies them the chances for the increases in consciousness, clarity, and empathy that frequently accompany difficulty.

Recognize these feelings of helplessness that are inspired by your Scarcity Groove fears. Empathize with the part of you that is terrified of losing even one degree of your child's full attention, love, and reliance upon you. Feel into the circumstances that may have caused your Scarcity Groove behaviors to develop, and shine love and light on those parts of you as you let them go.

Focusing on fear-driven hypotheticals prevents you from truly connecting with and honoring your child's autonomous path toward eventual independence. You also greatly risk damaging or undermining multiple aspects of their abilities to relate to the wider world without developing their own fears of scarcity. You are diminishing their capacity to reach their full potential as sovereign beings.

Discover you have a choice before you. A choice to act differently.

Also inherent to parenthood is the infinite potential for the greatest joy, wonder, discovery, connection, and love any human can experience. You as a parent are charged simply with loving your child without condition and providing reasonable guidance, security, and safety. From the moment they are born, imagine your child is embarking on their own personal and potentially amazing journey of discovery as they choose their own paths. Your job is to provide them with a consistent safe harbor to which they can return for reassurance, unconditional love, and reconnection as they course correct and continue along. Your job is not to steer their ship when your Scarcity Groove fears arise.

Imagine trusting your child to make their own choices, their own mistakes, and experience their own triumphs. Experience the deep curiosity of not knowing exactly how your beloved child's experiences will manifest as you let the circumstances of their autonomous lives unfold. You are there to cheer them on, help them recover, and love them, always love them, regardless of the paths they walk.

Feel how your own freedom and liberation increases as you let go of the exhausting and damaging role of the micromanager.

To be clear, parenting requires much hands-on caregiving, especially in the early years, to meet your child's basic needs. However, even from infancy, every choice you make as a parent can be grounded in your cultivated connection to your own guidance, thereby avoiding the fear-based micromanaging behaviors inspired by your beliefs in the Scarcity Groove.

Katie: Recognizing Destructive Behaviors as an Overscheduler

Following her lukewarm interview, Katie does the unthinkable. She calls in sick to her local hosting job, knowing the back-up host will likely be thrilled at the very rare opportunity to be on camera. Katie crawls back into bed and cries, feeling the fear of losing out to others threaten to overtake her. But she is also so exhausted and spread so thin that something inside of her lets go. Katie's physical, mental, and emotional exhaustion have reached a fever pitch and Katie has a moment of absolute clarity: she cannot continue her overwhelming schedule and still retain her health or sanity. She is turning in poor performances at all her jobs, she does not enjoy the opportunities she has, and her overscheduling tendencies may have just cost her a chance to be a correspondent on a national show. Katie finally understands that her fear of losing out is causing behaviors that will lead to her actually losing out.

With some trepidation, Katie pulls out a notebook and starts to make a list of the areas in her life that exhibit clear abundance. She is financially secure, she has a job entertaining people, she has a big, fun, loving family with whom she enjoys spending time, she has friends, some of whom are meaningful and nurturing, and others who are not. She delineates between these friends, making lists of those she can let go and those worthy of her time investment. She spends the entire day making lists and sorting through what would need to change if she were to build more ease and happiness in her life.

At the end of her very illuminating day, Katie crafts an email to the network executives, and explains about the late event she had worked the night before and requests a second meeting in a few days to better showcase her skills and potential. To admit to doing less than her best and advocating for a second chance is very scary, but Katie feels strongly it is the right move.

The executives agree to another meeting in a few days. Katie cancels the two events she is supposed to host in the intervening days, recommending competent replacements from her TV station who she knows will be thrilled at the opportunities. She carefully prepares and turns in an outstanding interview performance, sparkling with her natural curiosity, engagement, and connection. Katie's true excellence shines through, and the network executives offer her the job. The job is not full-time, but she cannot take this job and keep doing her daily local TV show every day. The idea of quitting her full-time local job, which is a safety net, fills her with anxiety. She approaches her bosses with the idea to share hosting duties with the back-up host. Thus, she can craft a schedule for travel and contributing to the network show while also keeping parts of her safe, local job. They agree. Katie eases out of many of her extra commitments and recommends her contacts and colleagues in the local entertainment industry as replacements.

Katie welcomes the new ease in her life and keeps up the practice of recording ways in which she experiences overflowing abundance in her life. She starts up a regular yoga practice, and she feels into her guidance as she moves through the poses, asking questions and letting her thoughts drift toward actions that feel most right. Sharing her local TV hosting duties frees her up to really concentrate and focus on the interviews she is responsible for with the network. Katie also tries hard to limit her assignments from the network, accepting those she can do well without becoming stretched too thin. She sometimes fails, taking on too many assignments for fear they will stop asking her, but the frequency with which she catches herself doing this increases and she gets better at saying yes only when it feels right.

Katie's natural talent for entertaining shines through more and more as she wastes less time frantically pursuing every avenue in her fear-motivated attempts to stay relevant and claim the spotlight. She finds she enjoys taking time to prepare and really connect with her interview subjects. The network executives recognize her potential and appreciate her preparation and engagement. Katie's extra time not only allows her to excel at her jobs but bring her added opportunities to feel into and connect with her guidance, not only during her yoga, but throughout the day, every day. She notices the increasing ease across all areas of her life and makes note of it in her journal. Katie has climbed out of her Scarcity Groove and embraced the way of her Guidance Groove.

In Conclusion

All behaviors arising from the fears motivating the Scarcity Groove are attempts to hold onto or attain what you perceive are insufficient resources, often at the expense of others. Thus, if the narrower examples provided do not exactly match your experience of the Scarcity Groove, you can use the flavor of the examples to further feel into how the Scarcity Groove may manifest in your life. Perhaps picture someone you know, or a fictional character or famous person, who fits one of the deeper examples of the Scarcity Groove. Relating in this way may help as you navigate your way out of your particular aspect of the Scarcity Groove.

Further steps for releasing from the Scarcity Groove, and the other Unproductive Grooves, are detailed in Chapter 7.

CHAPTER 6

The Unworthy Groove

Fear Motivator: You are afraid others will discover how worthless you are.

The **Unworthy Groove** is created and sustained when you believe certain aspects, or perhaps all, of your being are without worth or value. Your perceived unworthiness causes intense shame, leading you to withdraw from the facets of life for which you feel undeserving to participate. You believe you are not good enough, beautiful enough, interesting enough, smart enough, etc., to merit the fundamental joys and opportunities available to others. You may try to pursue attainment of life's prospects, but you consciously or unconsciously sabotage yourself in ways that prevent you from achieving even modest ambitions.

You frequently choose to remain without connection to inherent goodness for fear others will discover your deep unworthiness. You cannot allow yourself to fully accept love, friendship, job opportunities, and other circumstances that could elevate your life, because you truly believe you do not deserve any of it. The shame of accepting goodness when you feel you don't deserve it is overwhelming enough to prevent you from even trying.

When you believe some or all of your essential self is repellent to others, you become terrified of joining fully with the kindness, joy, connection, and beauty around you. Your shame at feeling so worthless overpowers the desire to connect with others in order to live a full, connected, rewarding life. You don't seek opportunities to improve, such as going to college, seeking a better job, living where you are most happy, or connecting with others in friendship or intimate love. Those things are for everyone else, for those who deserve acts of goodness. When someone manages to break through and reach out, you don't believe the sincerity of those overtures and often reject them because you are so mired in your spiral of worthlessness.

Aspects of the Unworthy Groove may seem to overlap with the Inadequacy Groove. However, the baseline drivers of each groove are different. Those in the Inadequacy Groove feel entitled to life's gifts and they pursue those goals. They are simply afraid their own perceived inadequacies will be discovered along the way, endangering their control of whatever they have achieved or want to achieve. Those stuck in the Unworthy Groove believe they are not entitled access to life's many rewards, and if they somehow achieve better, they reject it for fear attainment will expose the shame associated with their deep belief in their lack of inherent value.

Ego component: Your ego, or self-worth, is very connected to protecting your shame. When you lean into your deeply held beliefs of worthlessness, you can justify your disconnection from the world. You believe your pre-emptive rejection of others is necessary to protect yourself from potential rejection by humanity in case they discover how truly unworthy you are. You justify your actions to push others away, avoid connection, and refuse opportunities for expansion and improvement by convincing yourself invisibility is necessary to survive. In doing so, you remove humanity's access to your talents, assets, and whatever other sparks of light you contain that would benefit others and yourself. Protection of your shame is more important than listening to your guidance and thus feeds your spiral of unhappy inauthenticity.

Ben: The Invisible Man

Ben is an accountant at a small firm. Despite earning more money than he needs, Ben chooses to own a very modest house in an affordable neighborhood, he takes the bus to work, and he rarely buys anything new or unnecessary. Ben prefers to dress in clothes that are plain and at least one size too large. He feels anything else draws undue attention and he is constantly seeking to deflect attention away from himself.

When he first began working at the accounting firm, Ben was regularly invited to lunch gatherings, after work drinks, and other social events. Unless it is absolutely required for work, Ben always declines such invitations and chooses to eat lunch at his desk, go straight home, and otherwise avoid social interactions with his colleagues. He can't believe anyone at work would want to befriend him and assumes that their overtures are acts of those who feel obligated to include him. He rarely makes eye contact with others and moves through his workday as if he wished he could become invisible. Consequently, his colleagues long ago stopped reaching out and they mostly ignore Ben unless they are working directly together. Nobody is mean or unkind, they simply follow his lead and pay him little attention.

Ben is an excellent accountant, but he has declined most opportunities that would allow him to advance within the firm. Ben believes those opportunities should go to others who probably work harder, are smarter, have families to support, and who deserve to move ahead. He believes he isn't bright enough or good enough at navigating the politics of the workplace to accept more responsibility, increased pay, more challenging cases, or a bigger office. Plus, the discomfort of receiving more attention or having to interact more with others strongly outweighs any fleeting desires to improve upon his working conditions.

Something in his upbringing or belief system long-ago convinced Ben that he carries an internal shame, and that shame is so vast as to make him feel entirely undeserving of advancement at work, kindness from colleagues, and almost all positive attention in his workplace. He doesn't even deserve to use his well-earned money for anything pleasurable or excessive. Ben is deep within the Unworthy Groove.

Self-talk Examples of the Unworthy Groove

"I am nothing."

"Nobody could love me."

"That job (or person, place to live, or any opportunity) is way too good for the likes of me."

"They won't want to be my friend as I have nothing to offer."

"This party would be more fun without me."

"I wish I were invisible."

"My lover/friend/family member would connect better with someone else."

"I am disgusting."

"I am ashamed of myself."

"I don't deserve good things in my life."

"If others could see what I'm really like, they would reject me immediately."

"Nobody will miss me if I'm not there."

Do You Recognize Yourself in the Unworthy Groove?

You avoid social occasions, preferring to remain out of sight and off anyone's radar.

You don't look at people or invite others to look at you. Your clothing and style are meant to hide you in the hope others will not notice you exist.

You secretly scorn the happy connections and typical light-hearted interactions demonstrated by those around you.

You reject overtures of kindness or friendship for fear closeness with others will expose your burden of shame.

You keep your talents a secret, for fear sharing your skills will invite further rejection when your worthlessness is discovered.

You are most comfortable contributing toward the success and happiness of others, believing them more worthy than you.

You accept only minimal recognition for your efforts, experiencing severe discomfort when you are fully recognized, appreciated, welcomed, and loved.

Manifestations of the Unworthy Groove in the Life Arenas

School/Work/Life-Path

You seek and remain within jobs, classes, and situations that do not challenge you or highlight your talents in order to remain hidden.

You are solitary, choosing to remain separate from others during breaks in the work or school day.

You openly or secretly disparage others, rejecting them before they can reject you.

You feel anger or resentment toward those who appear to act without shame in their interactions with the world.

You reject accolades, appreciation, and recognition for jobs well done.

You sabotage successful situations rather than risk exposure as worthless and undeserving.

Family

Parent to Child

You push your unworthiness onto your children, causing them to feel shame about their own experiences.

You reject the natural, pure love of your children, allowing just enough, but not too much.

You accept degrading and disrespectful behavior from your children.

Grown Child to Parent

You reject overtures of connection, love, help, and care from genuinely loving parents, believing yourself unworthy to accept even a parent's love.

You continue to interact with non-loving parents even though their behaviors actively contribute to your feelings of worthlessness.

You hold your parent's shame and unworthiness as your own, hiding it to protect them from exposure.

Siblings

If your worthlessness stems from a shared familial experience, you guard the shame with your siblings to protect your family.

You feel envy toward siblings who don't exhibit signs of worthlessness.

You try and create feelings of unworthiness within your siblings, so you don't feel left alone with your shame.

Close Intimate Relationship

You only seek love partners who appear to carry more worthlessness and shame than you.

You never seek intimate partnership because that is only for worthwhile people.

You accept overtures for intimacy from belittling, shaming, critical, and unkind people because their hostility is what you deserve.

You cannot be fully present during sexual encounters, nor can you fully receive pleasure and connection with your sexual partners.

You may be able to give sexually but receiving is difficult or impossible.

You love others with lavish attention and care but cannot fully accept or believe in the love others offer you.

Friendship

You have few or no close friends and not many friendly acquaintances.

You connect with those who share your lack of worth, creating partnerships wherein you feed each other's stories of shame.

You avoid overtures of friendship and inclusion.

You rarely extend yourself in a friendly way toward others, choosing to remain as hidden as possible.

You are overly giving, generous, and attentive with friends, but expect, welcome, or accept little to nothing in return.

Community

You reject inclusion within your wider community, eschewing participation in neighborhood gatherings, church get-togethers, and other community building activities.

You strive for invisibility within your community, choosing to remain hidden and solitary.

You secretly scorn those who attempt to create and sustain wider connection within the community.

Examples

If you are stuck in the Unworthy Groove in any of the life arenas, your behaviors may reflect some of the shorter suggestions above. To better understand how you may be stuck, here are some deeper examples.

Ghosts wish to remain invisible to peers, colleagues, classmates, and family and you feel as if your survival depends upon this invisibility. You rarely speak or interact with those around you, even when you are invited to connect. You develop a physical appearance designed to repel attention. You, the ghost, cultivate a life of quiet obscurity, avoiding deep connections with others and potentially rewarding opportunities to thrive in your vocations because you believe even typical levels of visibility will expose your deep unworthiness and shame. Ghosts are not the same as those of you who are naturally introverted or shy. If you prefer your own company or have a tendency toward smaller social interactions, that is not the same as adopting the extreme invisibility that ghosts desire.

Ben: Living like a Ghost to Prevent Discovery of His Perceived Shame

Despite Ben's avoidance of most people in his everyday life, and especially at work, he has a group of people with whom he regularly relates via communities set up around his favorite video games on a chatting app. Ben has no reticence in relating to these people and he participates frequently in online gaming with individuals from these groups. These are

Ben's friends, and he feels welcomed and safe within the virtual spaces they have created. Occasionally, one or another of the groups suggests an in person meet up, but he always declines, and nobody pushes him to join.

That changes when Ben increases his chats with one person in particular named Charlotte. Over the course of many months, Charlotte becomes Ben's closest thing to a best friend, and he confides more in her than he ever has in anyone. Ben discovers he likes sharing more openly with another human and he looks forward to messages from Charlotte and she is equally effusive in her kind, friendly, and frequent exchanges with Ben.

Eventually, Charlotte tells Ben that he has become her very best friend and she cares for him and appreciates him in her life more than any of her other friends. She asks Ben if they could meet in person to further their friendship and even investigate if they could become more than friends.

Ben sincerely cares for Charlotte and has come to depend upon her easy friendship. For the first time in his life, he wants to push past his comfort zone and reach out to allow Charlotte greater personal access to him, including meeting her in person. But Ben imagines that somehow seeing him in person will allow Charlotte to know and feel his great internal shame, and that fear is so great, that Ben turns her down. Charlotte is confused because Ben has been so kind and open, so she gently presses Ben to explain further why he won't choose to meet up with her. He has no idea what to say and, rather than risk losing her completely as a friend once she discovers how unworthy he is, he replies that he doesn't have extra time to give her, and he thinks they should reduce their time spent chatting.

Charlotte feels some frustration and confusion. She is sincerely offering deeper connection to a man she perceives to be a wonderful human worthy of her time, care, and friendship. Luckily, Charlotte doesn't create a false story around Ben's withdrawal, but instead allows him to have his experience. When she responds, Charlotte explains that she hopes they can remain friends, but she says that she will pull back and, in the interest of her own self-preservation, she will consciously work to interact with him less to better respect his wishes. Once their interactions decrease, Ben discovers he misses Charlotte, her kindness, her caring, open way, her humor, and the easy way in which they related. He misses playing their favorite video games together and misses checking in with her throughout the day. Ben's discomfort at losing his best friend is so great that it finally causes him to pause and really examine his approach to interacting with others.

Givers provide lavish love, gifts, attention, and care upon lovers and friends, while remaining unable to fully accept love, recognition, and care from others. You support and facilitate excellence for your colleagues at work or school, devoting yourself to bolstering others without receiving adequate recognition or reward for your own contributions. Your continual sacrifices divert attention away from your own perceived unworthiness, while also allowing you to remain at a low level of appreciation, which is all you think you deserve.

Settlers make do with less-than-ideal friends, intimate partners, or other circumstances. You accept another person's mild interest or tepid opportunities, not expecting more, because you don't believe you deserve better. You actively avoid working toward or cultivating people and situations that would elevate your circumstances. You put up with and accept disagreeable behaviors from others and undesirable situations. You accept your nonideal circumstances and the crumbs of attention or minimal rewards offered by your partners, friends, and life circumstances, convinced these small offerings are enough. You believe that expecting more from life is only for those who are worthy, and that does not include you.

Initial Steps to Quit the Unworthy Groove

To free yourself from the Unworthy Groove, you must first recognize when your behaviors arise from your belief in this groove. Review the examples above. *Realize every behavior related to this Unproductive Groove is a choice.* When you act in ways to hide yourself, deflect attention toward others, excessively contribute to the well-being of those around you while ignoring your own needs, or in any way accept much less from life, *stop.*

Recognize the choice in front of you.

Set your objective to choose an outcome rooted in benevolent intentionality.

Notice and question the validity of every thought and belief that serves to reinforce your Unworthy Groove. You make the decision to consider yourself unworthy or not. You make the decision to consider yourself invisible or not.

Ask yourself:

"Do I need to take action (go for a walk, meditate, etc.) so I can better find, hear, and connect with my inner guidance?"

"How do I feel when I thoroughly disconnect myself from the rest of humanity?"

"Do I avoid other people for fear they will discover my deep worthlessness?"

"Do I avoid letting people get to know me for fear they will discover the aspects of myself of which I am ashamed?"

"Do I accept intimate partnership or friendship with those who mistreat me because I don't deserve better?"

"Do I actively sabotage situations in which I may thrive?"

"Do I feel disgust, scorn, dislike, or hatred for any aspect of myself?"

"Do I reject the affections of those I deem more worthy or otherwise better than me?"

"What would it feel like if I loved the parts of myself that I deem unworthy?"

"What would it feel like if I allowed others to fully love the parts of myself that I deem unworthy?"

"What is my internal guidance telling me?"

"What choices can I make to serve the best and highest good?"

Choose to love yourself. Find the parts of yourself that created and still carry stories of worthlessness. Is there a child within you who was repeatedly made to feel worthless by a parent or other authority figure while you were growing up? Did a lover or spouse leave you for someone else? Were you ever told you don't measure up, you aren't good enough, you will never succeed? Recognize how those experiences could contribute to a belief you are unworthy. Love the parts of you that carry your stories of worthlessness. Imagine those parts of you as dear friends or beloved children as that may help you give yourself the empathy, care, and gentle love you would extend toward those you care about. Actively loving those pieces of yourself will open the door to accepting love, care, and goodness from others.

Choose to forgive yourself. If your thoughts of worthlessness stem from an incident in which you did something truly wrong, causing shame, it is important that you empathize with and forgive yourself. Reach out and apologize to those you wronged. If that is not possible or they can't or won't forgive you, then seek absolution from yourself. Feel into your guidance to better understand your actions and to discover how best to make amends.

Choose to forgive others. Your earliest loved ones may have created or contributed to your Unworthy Groove. Perhaps your parents, siblings, or other family members consistently shamed you as a child, creating an ingrained belief in your innate worthlessness. Find compassion for their limitations and recognize they likely struggled with beliefs in their own lack of worth. Forgiving their egregious behaviors does not necessarily mean inviting them back into your life, but it frees you to fully let them go.

Choose to release unwarranted shame. Perhaps you were made to believe you did something wrong, but, upon reflection, you realize you did not. Be clear if the shame you carry stems from something you did that requires absolution or arose because someone made you falsely believe you did something wrong. Perhaps your worthlessness stems from some aspect of your innate humanity that you were taught is shameful. You were told you don't measure up to the expectations of others. Maybe you weren't "manly" enough, or you held sexual feelings deemed deviant by your community, or you weren't beautiful or smart or strong enough. Recognize how others' failed expectations reflect their own fears and shame. These are not yours to carry, so you can let them go.

Once you become more free of the burdens associated with the Unworthy Groove, look around and see if you notice a couple of things. First, if you sense a potential friend is offering you a place in their life, practice letting them in. Second, if you recognize the Unworthy Groove behaviors in others, take a moment to remember what it feels like to believe you are unworthy and perhaps you can reach out to them with clarity, kindness, and benevolent intentionality. Escaping this groove has provided you with a unique empathy and understanding that could be shared with others. You can now use what you have learned to extend the potential of greater freedom to those still stuck in the Unworthy Groove.

Deeper Examples that Show How to Leave the Unworthy Groove

Let's return to the previous examples to better understand practical ways to notice the choices before you, connect with your guidance, then act from love instead of fear. As with the other grooves, these examples are aspects of behaviors that manifest from your beliefs in the Unworthy Groove. While the exact labels (ghost, giver, settler) are different, the flavors or essences underlying the behaviors are similar and thus connected.

The Ghost in the School/Work/Life-path Life Arenas.

As a ghost, you wish to hide the aspects of yourself which you consider shameful. Those with whom you interact may seem friendly or kind, but you don't believe or welcome their sincerity. The interactions with others required for a minimal existence at work, school, or in any aspect of daily life, are difficult and fraught with unhappiness because you are constantly striving to remain inconspicuous. Your continual efforts to hide yourself are futile attempts to control your experience and the experience of everyone you meet. If you lose this control, it feels like you won't survive.

Imagine if you realized nobody was rejecting you without your express invitation and permission for their rejection. By insisting upon invisibility, you, the ghost, proactively spurn everyone first rather than risk rejection by others. And you are convinced rejection will occur if anyone gets close enough to uncover your worthlessness. Choosing to remain isolated as a ghost feels less painful than others choosing to isolate you.

Your concealment as a ghost is a comfort, but you sometimes yearn for closeness and you experience acute loneliness. You wonder what it would be like to be free of your shame, free to look others in the eye, free to be witnessed, acknowledged, welcomed, and seen by the people around you. Free to share your gifts with the world and be accepted and recognized as the vital, contributing, and beautiful being you are.

Follow that curiosity. Feel into it. What would it feel like to be truly seen?

You will remain a ghost, unseen to others, until you see yourself. Look hard and find those parts of yourself that you have consistently labeled unworthy. Treat those parts with empathy and care. Imagine those parts as small children, feel what it would be like to protect those children from unwarranted shaming. Feel love, compassion, and care for those parts of yourself that carry stories of worthlessness. Reassure all the parts of you that mistakes are normal and they are continual opportunities from life for increased learning, growing, compassion, and forgiveness.

To be truly without worth means you believe you have no value, nothing to offer yourself or humanity. Does your very existence fit that definition? *Absolutely not.*

Go back to the quote by the teacher Adyashanti at the beginning of Chapter 1. Every single being, every single living thing, has an "inner spark of radiance," including you. The beautiful light within you may be concealed by piles of debris built up by years of false beliefs in worthlessness, but you can clear them out so your light shines. Clear one small piece at a time, or perhaps huge chunks at once, until nothing blocks your luminance.

Instead of falling into your automatic urge to disappear, *stop*. Take a deep breath. Recognize the opportunity to choose a different reaction. Does withdrawing from humanity serve the best and highest good? For you? For those around you? Your co-workers, fellow students, and all you encounter? When you reflect on whether your existence fits the definition of worthless, what does your guidance tell you?

Listen to your guidance and tap into your own growing messages of worth, love, compassion, understanding, and belonging. Make lists or drawings or other impressions of ways in which you offer value to the Earth and humanity, no matter how small they seem. Each item added to the growing list of your own significance counteracts the false stories holding you in the Unworthy Groove.

Take manageable steps to reveal yourself. First to yourself. Your lists will help you see the many ways in which you add value to yourself, this planet, and other people. Then practice shining your light in the presence of others. Look a stranger in the eye and smile. Greet a co-worker with a simple "good morning." Accept an invitation to join someone for coffee or extend an offer to a friendly colleague for a lunch time walk. When someone compliments you, say thank you, let it sink in, accept that you are worthy of recognition.

Do not look to others to prove your worth. You have the power to connect to your own pure truth declaring your worth. Create, amplify, and consistently follow that truth. Each time you find yourself wanting to vanish, feel into your guidance, listen to the truth of your intrinsic worth calling from your ever-brightening spark of radiance, and *believe it*.

Ben: An Online Friendship Helps Ben Discover His Worth

Several weeks pass with very few exchanges between Ben and his former online best friend Charlotte. The discomfort at hurting her and the melancholy he feels when he thinks of all he misses by choosing not to interact with her increases. Finally, in a moment of clarity, Ben reaches out to Charlotte and asks for another chance. He explains that it's difficult for him to accept kindness from others and he is starting to suspect this difficulty is related to something that happened to him repeatedly in childhood that introduced, then reinforced, his belief that he was not worthwhile and didn't deserve basic goodness in his life. He asks if he could share his experience with Charlotte.

Reaching out to Charlotte and even hinting at his internal shame is the single scariest and most brave thing Ben has ever done. It takes all his courage and will to send this vulnerable message to Charlotte. He is sick with the fear of it, but soon, a response arrives. Not only is Charlotte happy to hear from Ben, but she is curious, understanding, empathetic, and willing to listen to Ben's admissions. They spend the next several days texting with more emotional intimacy than Ben has ever experienced with another human. Charlotte encourages Ben to seek a therapist who specializes in childhood trauma and helps him research practitioners in his area. He agrees and starts seeing the therapist regularly. He also starts walking every day at lunch for at least 30 minutes and he reflects on the advice from his therapist, reaching into himself to find his voice—the voice—that helps him decide if the stories he has long told himself about his unworthiness are even true.

Throughout these months of expansion, healing, and understanding, Ben and Charlotte grow closer and, when Ben shyly asks if Charlotte would still like to meet in person, he is mostly excited and happy when she agrees. Ben continues to follow the advice of his therapist, walking almost daily, and he takes up journaling to record his progress at escaping from his false beliefs in his lack of worth. He starts to pay attention to his colleagues and finds out more than one shares his love of a particular online game. They begin talking regularly when they pass each other in the halls and even have lunch together on a semi-regular basis. When his boss approaches him with a proposal for a harder case that will require more responsibility and a clear opportunity for advancement, Ben accepts and is soon promoted.

It's been a year since he reached out to Charlotte and Ben reflects on the many entries in his journal chronicling his growth and slow escape from the Unworthy Groove. With each entry, Ben's resolve to find, listen to, and trust his guidance increases and he feels joy at the progress he has made as a human relating to other humans. He is worthy of their attention, care, respect, and even love. Charlotte and he remain the best of friends and he is careful to thank her for her role in helping him realize his inherent worth. Ben feels increasing ease and contentment as he continues to develop his Guidance Groove.

The Giver in the Close Intimate Relationship Life Arena

You, the giver, are driven to provide for others, especially your lover, often to the detriment of your own well-being and satisfaction. You feel you do not deserve the full gifts of love from your intimate partner, so you put your efforts into satisfying their needs and wants. You offer abundant words and actions of love, but you are uncomfortable when your lover returns that level of ardor toward you. You believe endless giving is the only mechanism by which you can build up enough "credit" with your lover to justify receipt of a small amount of love in return.

You, the giver, may enact this Unworthy Groove in multiple ways across your partnership. You strive to please your lover sexually, lavishing him or her with attention, while taking only crumbs of pleasure in return. You consider your lover's career, friends, hobbies, children, home, or any aspect of their lives to be much more important than yours, giving energy and time to their pursuits, while neglecting your own. You actively reject enthusiastic, loving, and positive words, deeds, and actions because you believe you don't deserve any of it.

To avoid the discomfort of receiving undeserved love and attention, you choose intimate partners who encourage your endless giving and are happy to mostly take from you. They are pleased by your willingness to always place their needs above yours and are grudging in their small acts of affection toward you. When you continually choose lovers willing to always take and rarely give, you deepen your commitment to the Unworthy Groove.

If you do connect with a partner who wants to love you equally, they will quickly tire of your endless parade of unreciprocated giving. They will discern that your urge to give is not driven by a clean and clear desire to serve and love another, but instead is a tool to distract and prevent your lover from fully connecting with and giving to you in return. They recognize that you are preventing true intimacy by rejecting their overtures of love, desire, and care. They may also misperceive your refusals of their overtures of love as a rejection of them, further negatively impacting the relationship. Thus, the actions arising from your beliefs in your unworthiness prevent you from fully welcoming and receiving potential outpourings of love from a lover who sees your worth and wants to celebrate it.

When you feel yourself acting reflexively to give to your lover, *stop*. Notice the real, underlying intentions of your generosity. Are you pouring affection and positive actions into their well-being while actively holding a barrier preventing full reciprocation? Are you convinced that the only way in which you deserve to receive small amounts of love, affection, and care from your lover is if you smother them with attention first?

Recognize these feelings. Empathize with the part of yourself holding the beliefs that you are not worthy to receive exuberant, joyful, and genuine love, affection, and physical touch. Realize that your drive to constantly give to your intimate partner without allowing equal reciprocation stems from false beliefs in shame and your own worthlessness. Find the source of that shame and bring it forth. Shine your own loving light on that part of yourself. Pour the openheartedness you normally reserve for your lover into that part of you that believes you deserve only crumbs of affection.

Discover you have a choice before you—a choice to act differently.

Spend time with whichever system (exercise, meditation, music, journaling, etc.) you have discovered and cultivated that leads you to better connect with your guidance. Practice feeling into your guidance. What messages do you receive? Your true spark of radiance, from which your guidance springs, never doubts your worth. Return to that place every single time you find yourself falling into your Unworthy Groove.

Once you understand that your over-zealous generosity toward your intimate partners is motivated from your beliefs in the Unworthy Groove, you can change your behaviors. Relating with your lover can entail genuine giving and receiving. The motivation to express love to your partner will arise from the love, gratitude, and wonder you feel for your partner, not from the belief that smothering them with munificence will justify your receipt of even a tiny amount of love. When you are clear in your motivation, and clear in your belief that you are worthwhile and as deserving of love as every other human, then the relating with your lover can become one of equality.

With your newfound clarity and realization that you are worthy to receive bountiful love, your lover may be thrown off balance by your willingness to accept love, affection, gratitude, and appreciation. If you have allowed them to give you so little for a long time, they may have no idea how to be a true partner to you when you suddenly recognize your own worth and thus expect a more reciprocal relating. If this is the case, and they are unable to mutually give and receive with equality, then you must protect your own light, hold your own worth in the very highest regard, and find loving partnership with someone else. Never again let yourself allow such disparity with an intimate partner.

In Conclusion

Behaviors arising from the Unworthy Groove are grounded in varying degrees of shame that cause you to reject positive overtures and reinforce your stories of worthlessness. The examples provide a narrower focus, but by following the underlying "flavor," each example can be expanded to fit your own personalized experience with whatever degree of worthlessness you experience that keeps you trapped in the Unworthy Groove.

Further steps for releasing from the Unworthy Groove, and the other Unproductive Grooves, are detailed in Chapter 7.

PART 3

Break Free and Be True

*In order to be genuinely happy
there is one and only one thing you need to do:
get deprogrammed, get rid of those attachments.*

Anthony de Mello,
Jesuit priest, mindfulness teacher, and writer

C H A P T E R 7

Release into the Guidance Groove

Thank you.

I am grateful for your motivation to feel into your guidance to clear your adherence to the Unproductive Grooves. I recognize and honor your commitment to this journey. I am proud of you for your sincere willingness to go inward, recognize destructive patterns, then discover and create your best way forward. In seeking every opportunity to live within your Guidance Groove, you are choosing to be that spark of light that radiates within each of us; you are casting aside all arguments with its love.

You are also increasing the ability of others to do the same. Your success at becoming less programmed by your Unproductive Grooves and more in tune with your Guidance Groove will have positive repercussions for everyone around you. That will build collective authenticity, contentment, and happiness until you, and all of us, have nothing but positive feedback loops in all arenas of life.

Isn't that exciting?!

Yes, it is.

Final Steps for Release from the Unproductive Grooves

When you follow the simplified steps for living within your Guidance Groove, you naturally release from the Unproductive Grooves. Recall from Chapter 1:

Steps for Creating and Sustaining Your Guidance Groove

Recognize there is a choice before you.

Set your objective to choose an outcome
rooted in benevolent intentionality.

Identify the path arising from your
source of true guidance.

Trust your guidance
and choose your actions accordingly.

If you miss the mark,
learn from your experience,
and try again.

Your journey—in which you choose to sincerely discover how your behaviors fit into the Unproductive Grooves, then follow the steps above to be more free—requires **willingness, sincerity, vulnerability, bravery, compassion, empathy,** and **commitment.**

You must have a **willingness** to choose this path and to look at all aspects of your life with a deep **sincerity** so you may fully understand how your behaviors and actions align with any of the Unproductive Grooves.

Willingness and sincerity require **vulnerability,** a readiness to be laid bare and without defense or artifice, to come out of hiding from yourself and truly investigate with honesty, clarity, and unvarnished truth how you and your behaviors may be in false alignment with Unproductive Grooves.

To conquer anything scary requires **bravery** and it can be intimidating to strip away all armor and expose your vulnerability. Fear drives your resistance to being vulnerable. You are afraid of what may happen once you allow complete vulnerability, but bravery helps you face your fears, and, with **compassion** and **empathy,** you can eventually let them go.

Finally, your **commitment** to a life of genuine authenticity, contentment, ease, and truth requires consistent and sincere inquiry inward to gain deeper insights into how your patterns and stories can derail you. Committing to, embracing, and fully living by this requirement of consistent, sincere self-inquiry allows for your continuation on the beautiful path of daily, hourly, minute by minute connection to the natural and genuine flow of your own Guidance Groove.

Fears

Fears drive the behaviors emblematic of each Unproductive Groove and these behaviors arise as forms of self-protection. The false veneers stemming from your misguided beliefs in the need for protection generate an illusion of control so you can think you have power over the flow of your life.

Those of you in the **Inadequacy Groove** are driven by the fear that your inadequacies, however real or imagined, will be discovered. If that discovery happens, you will be vulnerable to exposure as a fraud and subsequent humiliation and rejection by others.

Those of you in the **Obligation Groove** remain committed to fulfilling false obligations because you are afraid you will be vulnerable to negative judgment when others label you as selfish and irrelevant for following your own guidance.

Those of you in the **Scarcity Groove** are afraid of missing out on vital resources. You believe you won't have enough emotional support, money, love, food, or security unless you grasp it and keep it from others. That way, you avoid becoming vulnerable to circumstance and other people's motivations and decisions.

Those of you in the **Unworthy Groove** are afraid that the shame stemming from your deep belief in your worthlessness will be uncovered. Discovery of your worthlessness will leave you vulnerable to contempt and banishment by humanity.

The specific fear drivers behind all the Unproductive Grooves can be simplified into this: You are afraid to be vulnerable.

You are afraid to be vulnerable to others. Vulnerable to their rejection, judgment, actions, and scorn. Vulnerable to the whims of others. To be vulnerable is to be without control and to dive into the unknown with no control can feel terrifying.

The old, Unproductive Groove way of thinking has led you to believe that constant control is the only way to get your needs met, but the Guidance Groove path teaches you otherwise. Letting go of your perceived control and instead acting from your continual internal guidance is a path to contentment. Trusting the flow of life, rather than trying to control it, will bring you more naturally into alignment with your unique Guidance Groove.

This doesn't mean you won't have a personality with preferences that influence your movement through the world and your interactions with others. It simply means you realize the preferences of others are just as valid as yours and trying to control all situations to protect yourself is unnecessary. In this way, your beautiful and unique personality can truly and freely shine without being hindered by fears, false beliefs, and endlessly exhausting attempts to control.

Releasing your Fears and Embracing your Guidance Groove

When you are ashamed of your fears, and do everything to avoid facing them, you tend to be harsh and critical, telling yourself your fears are bad, weak, and must be banished. If you choose to ignore your fears, they will never, ever let you go. Instead, embrace your fears, move toward them, analyze them, work to understand where they come from, and why they are not true. Your fears are valuable clues that help you better understand which of your behaviors are driven by your adherence to one or more of the Unproductive Grooves.

You can learn to recognize your fears as precious indicators that are designed to help you escape into the Guidance Groove. You will increasingly realize that your fears are simply false beliefs that have outgrown their usefulness, and you can treat them with the same compassion that you would treat the unfounded fears expressed by a child or other loved one. Then you are more able to face your fears, love them, and gently let them go. The compassion and empathy you extend to yourself in this process will build, allowing you to extend that same loving understanding to all around you.

Learn to talk kindly to yourself in ways that help you break down your fears and prevent your fears from creating and deepening your Unproductive Grooves. Remind yourself that certain, Unproductive Groove-inspired actions may be harmful or not serving the best and highest good, but do not shame yourself. Gently, firmly, lovingly hold yourself accountable without creating unnecessary and destructive self-talk. Maybe you had parents who treated you in a loving way when you needed course correction as a child, so you have excellent examples.

Maybe you have no examples of this in your immediate life. Maybe you don't have a trusted friend, parent, or loved-one to remind you of your myriad strengths and absolute lovability. For those of you, it is especially important that you learn to talk kindly to yourself. If, at first, you cannot do this, then practice talking to yourself as you would to your most revered loved-one or an innocent child seeking guidance.

Once you can talk kindly to yourself, you start to recognize, deepen, and grow your own *true love*. You may have lost sight of it, but this love has always existed within you and always will. Connect with it, build it, and learn to immerse yourself in your own true love. This true love is whatever you define it to be, and you can never lose it. It will always be with you, regardless of circumstances. That deep true love will hold you dear even in the face of your faults and shortcomings. The benevolent intentionality to choose outcomes for the best and highest good comes from this place of true love. Feeling into, acknowledging, and trusting that true love helps you identify and trust your own guidance. You can then more easily choose actions based on your guidance which allows for more alignment with your own authenticity. You'll experience more freedom, more happiness, more ease.

Forging new types of connection with your co-workers, bosses, friends, intimate partners, children, parents, or anyone, in the open, vulnerable, and unguarded manner required for living within your Guidance Groove may initially seem scary. Again, don't run from the fears that may arise as you relate more authentically with others. Welcome them, take a good look, feel into them. Ask yourself—are these fears even true? Love yourself through the fears as you release them. Continually inquire as to which outcome serves the best and highest good as you relate with those around you. Your guidance and sincere inquiry will help you discover choices that are rooted in benevolent intentionality. And, if you miss the mark as you build new ways of connecting with the humans around you, then you simply forgive yourself and try again.

As you live more in accordance with your Guidance Groove, your discomfort at living outside of your authenticity will increase until that discomfort is much stronger than your fears of exposing yourself as vulnerable. *This is very important*: making choices rooted in Unproductive Grooves becomes increasingly uncomfortable the more you choose to live a life in alignment with your Guidance Groove. Once this tipping point occurs, then you will automatically choose to do the "scary" things in order to remain aligned with your inner guidance and true authenticity. This is because living any other way is unbearable.

Michael and Anna: Creating an Intimacy Guidance Groove Together

Michael loves his wife Anna for her beauty, intellect, quick wit, and kindness, yet at some level, he has always felt entirely separate from her, as if there is a seemingly unbridgeable chasm between them, and he longs for deeper closeness and easy intimacy. Their sexual chemistry has always been high, and they frequently make love, but he suspects that his longing for greater connection with the woman he loves dearly is thwarted by how they make love. His guidance is telling him he must talk with Anna to better discover what they can do as a couple to increase their relationship authenticity, closeness, and ready intimacy.

Anna lavishes Michael with compliments, romantic gifts and gestures, and she takes a very active role in the bedroom. She is intent on his pleasure, focusing her attention on exciting Michael, always performing the actions that she knows will bring him to climax.

At the start of their relationship, Michael welcomed Anna's singular attention, reveling in the many ways Anna sought to enhance his sexual pleasure and demonstrate her affection. However, when he attempts similar reciprocation, Anna becomes less animated, more closed down, and she has never welcomed or encouraged his attempts to pleasure her. She turns the attention back to Michael or explains that it is difficult for her to climax or, Michael increasingly suspects, she pretends to orgasm to end the lovemaking after Michael is satisfied.

Anna is deep within the Unworthy Groove when it comes to relating sexually with her beloved Michael. She loves him deeply, but as a child, she was taught sex is dirty, something only "bad" girls did, embedding the shame of sexual pleasure deep within her being from a very early age. It was fine to pleasure a man, because she was taught the man in her life would leave if she didn't please him sexually, but it was shameful for her to find pleasure from her actions and from her own sexuality.

Michael feels into his guidance, reflecting carefully on the messages Anna sends when she rejects his efforts to increase her pleasure, thereby rejecting his attempts to create deeper connection and intimacy between them. His intuition leads him to suspect Anna's refusal to accept more than minimal sexual attention is rooted in shame and protecting this shame from growing unmanageable requires her to refuse most personal physical pleasure from her husband.

This is valuable information, but only half the equation. Michael also deeply feels into his own equal part in allowing their lopsided sexual interactions to continue for far too long without comment. What Unproductive Grooves prevent Michael from asking for and experiencing the emotional and physical shared intimacy he craves from the wife he loves? In reflection, Michael discovers he feels insufficient to the task of fully satisfying his partner, so he goes along with her excessive ministrations, allowing him to turn a blind eye to his own fears of inadequacy. He also feels obligated to protect the status quo of their relationship, so he avoids potential conflict or distress by ignoring a sensitive topic. Finally, Michael believes that the type of closeness he craves is scarce, and potentially impossible to experience, with Anna or with anyone else.

Even after Michael has fully formed his Guidance Groove-led theories, he avoids talking with Anna. He is fearful of confrontation, worried he will upset her, and uncomfortable with bringing up such a delicate topic. But mostly Michael is scared Anna will dismiss his concerns and they will never achieve the closeness he craves. This fear of scarcity seems easier to live with than the potential confirmation of the scarcity that might happen if he approaches Anna, makes himself vulnerable, and asks for what he needs.

Finally, when Michael starts to fantasize about the closeness he could potentially achieve sexually and emotionally with other women who are not his wife, he knows it's time to talk with Anna. The discomfort he feels living within the situation with Anna has become stronger than his discomfort in bringing up the topic. He plans for a moment when they are alone, quiet, rested, and free from distraction.

Michael is careful to be loving and kind. He explains to Anna that she is his beloved and he longs for an intimacy that he believes would permeate all aspects of their relationship if they were truly reciprocal and fully open in their loving of one another in the bedroom. He explains how much he loves her willingness to be sexually exciting with him, and he asks if they could try some experiences where the focus is on Anna's pleasure. Michael comes completely out of hiding and freely owns and shares with Anna his responsibilities for co-creating their current situation. He makes himself vulnerable and explains his fears and how he may be stuck in one or more Unproductive Grooves when it comes to relating sexually with Anna. He gently asks what Anna feels in response to his revelations and wonders if she feels shame around her sexuality. He expresses concern, understanding, and a willingness to both continue exploring his own actions that have prevented further intimacy and to help Anna discover whatever might be holding her in Unproductive Groove behaviors.

Anna is horrified at first. The conversation with Michael is uncomfortable, and, despite Michael's best efforts to be kind and gentle, she feels accused of being cold and withholding, when all she's ever done is try her best to please Michael as a lover. Her defenses are up, and she feels scared, as if she has done something wrong and is being called out.

But she also loves Michael and knows that he truly loves her. That love shines through her fear and allows her to take a moment, pause, and really listen to her lover. In requesting reciprocal intimacy, Michael is asking for her to be vulnerable to him. He is also offering to be vulnerable to her, expressing his willingness to explore his own Unproductive Grooves and make them more shallow or nonexistent together. He wants to pleasure her, wants to help relieve her burden of shame over her sexuality, wants to spend the time working together to increase their intimacy. He wants to show her how much he loves her, freely, without boundaries and walls, with an easy back and forth that leads to mutual pleasure and release. Michael wants that foundation of intimacy to permeate all aspects of their life together and he believes true, open, loving, and reciprocal sexuality is a key.

Anna discovers she yearns for that closeness as well but does not know how to achieve it. She feels into Michael's gentle suggestions that she may believe she is unworthy to receive pleasure and these beliefs may stem from feelings of shame that were ingrained into her sexuality from an early age. This resonates deeply with her, and she recognizes their truth. She works with Michael to uncover those feelings and bid them farewell. Michael supports her efforts, seeking his own help from her to discover why he accepted his unhappiness with their sexual relating for so long.

Over time, with lots of practice, patience, curiosity, and fun,

Anna and Michael build a new chapter in their shared sexuality. It feels stilted and programmed at first, but eventually, they come to a place where they naturally move back and forth, taking turns pleasuring one another, reveling in the discoveries of unboundaried lovemaking. The close intimacy they have built in the safe, loving exploration of their shared sexuality permeates other aspects of their relating, increasing the depth of their verbal communication and helping smooth most edges that arise. They work to build a mutual intuition experience and soon it is no work at all. They naturally flow within this experience for every nuance, every choice, every touch as they move and grow together in their evolving, ever-deepening intimacy Guidance Groove.

Living in your Guidance Groove requires you to *trust your intuition and guidance*. Authenticity, connection, joy, and ultimate freedom can be achieved if you trust your choices to live in alignment with your inner guidance and truth. Practice connecting with your guidance and learn to trust it. Then notice when trusting in your guidance brings release, ease, and greater happiness. Keep track of those times by writing them down. Accumulating evidence of positive outcomes that occur when you choose to live within your Guidance Groove will help you to build greater trust in your guidance.

As you work to restructure or leave relationships or situations created by adherence to any of the Unproductive Grooves, *accept the potential discomfort* you may feel when others believe you are disloyal or unkind for following your truth. Think back to the allegory of leaving the ravine in Chapter 2. Escaping from the muck at the bottom of the ravine is difficult, especially when others pull you back in response to their rising fears. Remain within your benevolent boundaries, act from love and guidance, then trust in the process. Once the dust settles, a life in which your choices are more in alignment with your own authenticity will lead to increased peace, freedom, happiness, and ease. For everyone. Because nobody can be truly content when they or those around them are immersed in lives of inauthenticity. And once you reach the airy freedom at the top of the ravine, you can turn and kindly shine your light on those who are still climbing.

If you truly want to be free of the Unproductive Grooves, you must be willing to risk others perceiving you as selfish. Remember, *insisting on alignment with your own truth when it is rooted in benevolent intentionality is not selfish.* We all must reexamine this paradigm and reject it. The feelings arising in others in response to you following your guidance are not your responsibility. You can be kind, gentle, empathetic, and careful as you make choices in alignment with your guidance, instead of following your own false stories and the stories and demands of others, but you do not have to manage the feelings and emotions of others. There are true selfish behaviors, of course. When we ignore the negative outcomes of our actions and refuse responsibility for our own choices, selfishness results. But actions arising from genuine benevolent intentionality and in service to the best and highest good, and applied with love and commitment to authenticity, are not selfish.

Commitment to escaping the Unproductive Grooves requires you to recognize when you have relapsed into the behaviors emblematic of the grooves. There may be pressures created by yourself and others to continue these behaviors that are familiar, known, and reliable. Remember, the people who love us, and who themselves act according to guidance from their own best and highest good, want us to maximize our potential and live our best, happiest, most authentic lives. If those around you act otherwise and try to pull you away from your own Guidance Groove, realize you cannot change them, only yourself. There is great power and freedom in making your own choices to escape the behaviors from the Unproductive Grooves.

If you do relapse or in any way act from your Unproductive Groove stories rather than your own guidance, please do not be hard on yourself. It's OK. We all miss the mark. None of us is perfect and living within your Guidance Groove is not about perfection. It is a moment by moment moving with the natural flow of your life from a place of maximum wholeness and authenticity. Every moment is a fresh chance to move with that flow. If your decision about something feels off, or the outcome is not what you envisioned, then you can simply recognize you have missed the mark. You can now lovingly feel into the choice before you and try again. One of the beautiful aspects of choosing to be in constant alignment with your Guidance Groove is that life continually provides you with endless chances to experiment with and experience the process of finding, trusting, and following your guidance. And with repetition comes improvement and proficiency.

Welcome an expression of *gratitude* for every time you recognize ways in which you are still following Unproductive Grooves. These are opportunities to practice the steps for following the Guidance Groove. Think back to the stories of Allen, Rachel, Katie, Ben, and Michael. None of them escaped from their Unproductive Grooves until their life circumstances became so unbearable that they were forced to really look into their behaviors and seek to make a change. In this way, life becomes your most valuable teacher, constantly providing opportunities to discover ways in which you can become increasingly free of Unproductive Groove behaviors.

The unease you feel when you are acting from inauthenticity helps you discover when you are out of alignment with your guidance. Sometimes you require a lot of discomfort from life in order to see, learn, change, and grow. But, as you become more aligned with your Guidance Groove, you don't need such intense pressure. You make choices in alignment with your own authenticity in response to even the smallest hint of discomfort. And the result is a feeling of peace and ease in your deepest self. Experiencing this profound relief is the signal that you are following your Guidance Groove.

Also recognize and be grateful for the many, many times you successfully connect with and follow your guidance. Living within your Guidance Groove is an ongoing process, and you are on a continual path that only becomes wider and longer the more you create, refine, and improve upon your beautiful, unique, exquisite Guidance Groove.

Be grateful you've found your Guidance Groove, that you even know it exists to follow.

Be aware *you may hold others in Unproductive Grooves* via your choices. As you work toward freedom from the Unproductive Grooves, ask yourself if you manipulate, pressure, and otherwise act in ways to hold others in any of the Unproductive Grooves. Recognize when your actions and choices may prevent others from most easily achieving their own freedom from the Unproductive Grooves. Then choose to act instead from your own authentic guidance. When we all make choices aligned with our own truth, then we can whole-heartedly support one another in our ongoing endeavors to remain authentic.

Perhaps most importantly, you must remember that living within your harmonious Guidance Groove requires you always to set your intentions for the best and highest good. You must apply this benevolent intentionality every single time you seek, listen to, and follow your guidance so as to avoid actively harming others.

Finally, there are some patterns and behaviors developed across a lifetime that have too strong a hold to be released with the tools presented in this book. There are professional mental health healers who can help you and I urge you to seek out and work with them if you find that working on your own or within your community is not enough. My former husband Christian and I found great wisdom, help, and clarity with the help of a fantastic therapist early in our relationship. We were not able to achieve that harmony through sincere, simple, and honest inquiry on our own. Working with the therapist, we acquired outstanding tools to relate more openly and lovingly with one another and better understand ourselves. Though we did not remain married, the work we did years ago with our therapist eased our path of relating so we are able to love one another in genuine familial friendship as we co-parent our son.

Conclusions

Making choices rooted in benevolent intentionality that are in alignment with your authenticity will feed and grow whatever serves as your own personal source of guidance and your connection with your guidance will become ever more expansive. When you set your benevolent boundaries, you protect your source of guidance, and you can then approach others with more consistent authenticity, empathy, kindness, and a firm understanding of the best action for the highest good. From there, you can choose the best outcomes in cooperation with others, and everyone can act from a place of love and mutual commitment to remaining aligned with each person's own guidance. Working together, we can make loving agreements to release one another from the Unproductive Grooves.

The more you share with others the joy experienced from living authentically in alignment with your guidance, the more we can all be working on these principles together, creating community and mutual support. Imagine how your homelife could be improved if everyone in your family was committed to acting in accordance with personal guidance that is in alignment with benevolent intentionality. Imagine if you all came out of hiding and talked with each other about your own processes, sharing successes and missed opportunities, encouraging the escape from Unproductive Grooves and cheering each other on as you progress. You and your family members would be free to be. Simply be your authentic selves. Free to be vulnerable, undefended, and without the false fears driving the Unproductive Grooves.

Now imagine what daily interactions with others would be like if commitment to the Guidance Groove extended to humans beyond your immediate family—to your extended family, friends, co-workers, neighbors, acquaintances, and strangers. Benevolent intentionality, alignment with guidance, and authenticity, freedom, contentment, ease, and increased happiness for all creates ever-expanding community Guidance Grooves that promote further societal harmony and unity.

We are all ready for greater authenticity, connection, and unity. Let us all welcome, create, foster, and promote this vision for everyone. Together, we can do this for ourselves and for each other.

Dearest Reader,

The Guidance Groove is not a self-improvement plan or a way for you to achieve your vision of perfection or live in endless, abiding happiness.

It is an invitation to discover how to increase your authenticity in your day-to-day interactions with all who cross your path.

It's about discovering that you don't have control over other people and circumstances, but you do have the power to make choices that are in alignment with your highest truth. You can approach all of life as a truly integrated and whole human, navigating circumstances while utilizing data from the thinking, feeling, and intuitive aspects of yourself.

And a byproduct of living within the flow of your personal alignment is greater ease, freedom, truth, and very possibly, happiness.

As you progress, realize that all circumstances within your life, especially those that are difficult, uncomfortable, or painful, are invitations to grow, learn, and rid yourself of false stories that do not serve you. You can embrace the painful situations in life, discover your part in their inception and continuation, learn when they are made-up constructs, then release your untrue thought patterns. The freer you become of these mental stories, the more your true, authentic, unguarded, unique, and whole self can shine. And living within your newfound authenticity will be a hugely positive contribution to yourself, those around you, and all of humanity.

Have fun and enjoy your experiences building, nurturing, expanding, and living by your own Guidance Groove. Collect your stories, then share your new-found path to authenticity, joy, and greater ease with others.

I look forward to joining you all in our collective community Guidance Groove.

With so much love, care, encouragement, and gratitude,

Carolyn

Acknowledgments

Thank you so very much to you, the reader who chose and read this book, who shared it with others, and who take its principles to heart for your daily practice of living within your own personal and gorgeous Guidance Groove. I'm in awe of your willingness and bravery.

So much gratitude to:

My editor—Mary Holden—you are a force of nature, a wonder to behold, and so very good at your job. I love how we found each other (the TBTL podcast!), and I am grateful for the work we get to accomplish together. You were instrumental in the production of this book and your help, enthusiasm, encouragement, and willingness has been so welcome and exactly right. I love the experience of our friendship and relating and I delight in your inspirations. You are dear to me and I thank you deeply.

My book designer—Anugito ten Voorde of Artline Graphics. You brought to life what was previously only a vision and I'm so grateful for your wise and artistic insights that created the interior and strengthened the cover of this book.

My team at Smith Publicity, Inc.—Courtney Link, Olivia McCoy, Corinne Moulder, Lydia Rassmusssen, Jessica Sager, and Janet Shapiro. Your expertise, enthusiasm, care, and outstanding support were invaluable in promoting and sharing this book.

My earliest readers—Martha Cantwell, Mike Curtin, Mary Hedgcock, Don Kurle, Tom Valente, Stan Vegar, and Marian Wolfe—your willingness to read early versions of this book and to be honest and clear with feedback was invaluable. Thank you so much for accepting that responsibility and for sincerely providing help to me.

My spring 2022 lab group—Danelle Baronia, Kelly Flanders, Tristie Le, Keeley Lanigan, Stephanie Nehasil, and Kara Reynolds. Your willingness to read and discuss an earlier version of my book was so kind and generous. The weekly input and feedback you all provided was absolutely invaluable to me and greatly improved the clarity, value, and meaning of the entire project. I deeply thank you for giving me your time and your incredibly useful and wise insights. You all continually amaze me and the experience of sharing this with you was instrumental for my own escape from certain groove behaviors.

My BIEB 194 Summer 2022 Seminar Students—Luke Aguon, Jillian Diamse, Daisy Flores, Kamonkan (Joy) Gamnerdsiri, Nathan Glonek, Emma Hong, Hairui (Hailie) Hou, Summer Khan, Marissa Knopf, Robina Shoukry, Helena Teir-Aguon, and Hanru (Esther) Zhou. Your commitment to open, vulnerable sharing and relating with me and each other was lovely to experience. The insights, feedback, and discussions of the material in the book were priceless in their value to me as an author and I am so grateful for the clarity and inspiration you provided that improved this book. Thank you for your willingness to embark on a wholly unusual biology seminar and for the kind, open, generous, supportive, and caring nature with which you co-created our shared seminar space.

My students—the undergraduates and graduate students at UC San Diego. I love teaching you, but I especially love how much I've learned from all of you. It's an honor to work with you and you all continually inspire me and fill me with so much faith in those younger than me. Thank you for being so kind, generous, brilliant, and full of earnest endeavors.

My inspirations—the musicians Krishna Das and Snatum Kaur provided the soundtrack for this phase of my life, especially throughout the writing of this book. And Adyashanti, whose wisdom and clarity on the process of becoming more free has been an illuminating force in my life for close to 20 years.

Trevor Jackson of TJ Biographies—the website you created for The Guidance Groove is beautiful. Thank you for your excellent work.

Kara Reynolds—you realized my vision for the book cover with elegance, seeming ease, and so much enthusiasm, expertise, and inspiration. I marvel at your wide-ranging abilities as an artist, seamstress/designer, event planner, writer, and scientist. I'm truly grateful you showed up in the first row of one of my classes years ago.

Thank you so much.

My friends—Dan Bregar, Joey Christy, Leslie Cornick, Kim Ferree, Peter Hinkley, Shawn Kuchta, Amy Martin, Sidney Merritt, Shari Pickett, Shauna Reisewitz, Jo Salatas, Gayle Valensky, Diana Steller, Emily Troemel, and Aimee Weber—and so many others. I'm consistently lucky to have the exact right people cross my path at the exact right times. Thank you to the many of you who have walked with me on that path when it has been our time to connect. I truly love all of you.

Christopher White—for so openly sharing your stories with me, teaching me to ride, and for allowing me to use your experiences as examples of what it means to follow guidance. Thank you, my friend.

Julie Jackson—Thank you for your encouragement to begin this project and for helping hone my earliest ideas. Thank you for challenging me, for your willingness to explore truth, and for sharing your expansive love. My deep honor, gratitude, and love to you.

David Kurle—Thank you for being my brother. I love you.

Jackie Kurle—Thank you for your insights and knowledge that helped me navigate the process of building an online presence. And thank you for being a friend, the beautiful mama to your dear Kurle kids, and a cheerleader for understanding and goodness.

Mary Ann Kurle—Thank you for being such an important part of my family and for your enthusiastic love and support over so many years. You are my mother/sister/friend, a kindred spirit, and a true gift to me and so many. I love you.

Steven Kurle—You have been deeply important to me from the moment you were born. Thank you for being my consistent, insistent, and patient teacher. I have learned so much as your sister and I love you and our connection.

Martha Cantwell—Thank you for everything. You have been my perfect guide and teacher since my inception, and your willingness, patience, faith, and unwavering love and acceptance of me are crucial to my well-being and growth as a human. I love you so much and I'm so lucky you are my mom.

Christian Marcotte—You are forever my family and the wonderful papa for our son. Thank you for all of it. I love you and our journey together and am eternally grateful for our beautiful, joined path.

J. Stanley Vegar—Thank you, darling, from the bottom of my heart for being my sounding board, my first reader, my open-minded, open-hearted, courageous, enthusiastic, and willing collaborator in exploring the vast expanse of intimate relationship, and for being an exactly perfect teacher for me. Your continued sincerity, bravery, vulnerability, and love are inspiring. I love you dearly.

Jeremiah Kurle-Marcotte—Thank you, Bugsy, for being my most exquisite teacher. That I get to call you son and serve as your mama is the biggest gift of my life. You are the best of the best. I love you.

References

Campbell, J. 2004. *Pathways to Bliss: Mythology and Personal Transformation. Novato*, CA. New World Library

Harris, S. 2014. *Waking Up: A Guide to Spirituality Without Religion.* New York, NY. Simon and Schuster.

Koydemir, S, Simsek, ÖF, Kuzgun, TB, and Schütz, A. 2020. *Feeling special, feeling happy: Authenticity mediates the relationship between sense of uniqueness and happiness.* Current Psychology 39:1589-1599

Robinson, GE and Barron, AB. 2017. *Epigenetics and the evolution of instincts. Science* 356(6333):26-27

Brown, B. 2018. *Dare to Lead.* New York, NY. Random House

NOTES

NOTES

NOTES

NOTES

NOTES

NOTES

NOTES

NOTES

NOTES

NOTES

NOTES